Praise for *Ingaging Leadership*

Having known Evan Hackel for more than 40 years, and personally observed his business acumen and personal commitment to enlightened approaches to executive leadership, I know that his thoughts on ingagement strategies ring true to his personal and professional true north. He has learned through the experience of numerous business challenges that understanding the "art" of human communication and organizational dynamics is absolutely key to overall business success. You may consider some of the concepts in this book absolute common sense, but you would be surprised how few people actually use them to their advantage. Don't be one of them.

> —Rear Admiral Bob Day, U.S. Coast Guard (retired), CIO and Cyber Commander, 2009–2014 and Principal at Bob Day & Associates LLC

Ingaging Leadership is a brilliant and masterfully written book. It is fantastic for any business or organization. Ingagement, attitude, and communication are the foundation stones for any organization. I've had the privilege to learn and experience Evan's leadership first hand as one of the Flooring America Dealers. The results have brought me huge success over the years. Evan is "The Real McCoy" and I can say that since I am a Hatfield.

> —Phillip Hatfield, Executive and Business Coach, Zig Ziglar Corporation

Ingaging Leadership is a timely and eminently practical book that will definitely help leaders to improve their ability to bring out the best in others. The strategies and case studies Evan Hackel shares are relevant to businesses of all shapes and sizes. I particularly gained a lot from the sections on how to improve personal communication.

—Greg Nathan, author of *Profitable Partnerships* and Founder, Franchise Relationships Institute

Ingaging Leadership

Ingaging Leadership

21 Steps to Elevate Your Business

EVAN HACKEL

Motivational PRESS
LEADERS IN GLOBAL PUBLISHING

Published by Motivational Press, Inc.
1777 Aurora Road
Melbourne, Florida, 32935

www.MotivationalPress.com

Copyright 2016 © by Evan Hackel
All Rights Reserved

No part of this book may be reproduced or transmitted in any form by any means: graphic, electronic, or mechanical, including photocopying, recording, taping or by any information storage or retrieval system without permission, in writing, from the authors, except for the inclusion of brief quotations in a review, article, book, or academic paper. The authors and publisher of this book and the associated materials have used their best efforts in preparing this material. The authors and publisher make no representations or warranties with respect to accuracy, applicability, fitness or completeness of the contents of this material. They disclaim any warranties expressed or implied, merchantability, or fitness for any particular purpose. The authors and publisher shall in no event be held liable for any loss or other damages, including but not limited to special, incidental, consequential, or other damages. If you have any questions or concerns, the advice of a competent professional should be sought.

Manufactured in the United States of America.

ISBN: 978-1-62865-304-5

For Paul Hackel

I dedicate this book to my father Paul Hackel, who passed away as this book was nearing completion in June, 2015. He was an inspiring man who allowed me to begin working for his company when I was only 10, affording me the opportunity to observe, admire and learn from him as he conducted business with the utmost care and dedication. To him I owe both my success and my love and knowledge of business.

Table of Contents

Foreword — ix

INTRODUCTION
What Is Ingagement About? — 1

CHAPTER ONE
What Is Ingagement? — 7

CHAPTER TWO
Does Ingagement Really Work? — 17

CHAPTER THREE
Practical Ways to Master the Art of Ingaged Management — 37

CHAPTER FOUR
Understanding and Communicating Your Company's Identity and Purpose — 67

CHAPTER FIVE
Communication Skills for Ingaged Leadership — 85

Table of Contents

CHAPTER SIX
    Mastering The Three Types of Communication   101

CHAPTER SEVEN
    Building a Strong and Ingaged Team   117

Conclusion   141

Epilogue to the Second Print Edition   145

Appendix A: Track Your Action Steps and Get Started   151

Acknowledgements   161

About the Author   167

About Ingage Consulting   169

About Tortal Training   173

About Ingaging Leadership...   175

Please Tell Me More   177

Index   179

Foreword

By Howard Brodsky,
Co-Founder, Chairman and Co-Chief Executive Officer, CCA Global Partners

Over the last 25 years, I have had the privilege to work closely with Evan Hackel. When Evan joined CCA Global Partners, we were a very small company. He was our fifth employee. Evan was very instrumental in helping the company grow to over 10 billion dollars in system-wide sales. Evan helped us expand and establish departments to manage Marketing, Training, National Programs, and Recruitment. He also helped us launch many new businesses, including ProSource Wholesale Floorcovering, Stone Mountain Outlet, Lender's One, Savvi Formalwear, Biking Solution and BizUnite.

Perhaps Evan's biggest accomplishment was leading our effort to turn around the Flooring America Franchise, which we bought out of bankruptcy. At that time, Flooring America was doing about $700 million in system-wide sales. Within four years with Evan as the executive in charge, Flooring America had achieved $2 billion in annual system-wide sales. Evan could never have been that successful without being the leader he is.

It has been great to watch Evan grow as a person and as leader. Early in his career, Evan wasn't the ingaged leader he describes in this book. But over time he evolved. It has been fun and inspiring to witness first-hand the evolution of his leadership. As a leader, Evan has not taken an easy path or focused solely on the day-to-day issues of doing business. He has, in fact, committed himself to the mastery of an ingaged leadership approach that has required him to seek a deeper understanding of himself, of the people he leads, and of the organizations where he and employees ingage with one another to create both sustainable profits and growth. I think that is remarkable.

In this compact book, Evan shares not only his philosophy of leadership, but also a range of reality-based, practical solutions that support it. His advice is concise, clear, actionable, easy-to-digest, yet powerful enough to help any leader quickly reach new levels of success.

I commend Evan for writing this book, and I recommend it highly.

INTRODUCTION

What Is Ingagement?

Even before you begin to read this book, you are probably wondering about why I chose the title "Ingaging Leadership" rather than "Engaging Leadership." If you visit a bookstore, you will find books about engagement. So why have I chosen to write a book about ingagement, not engagement? What is the difference?

The first difference is that the word ingagement cannot be found in dictionaries. The word engagement can. If you look it up, you will find definitions like these:

- A commitment to be somewhere for a designated period of time.
- A formal agreement to get married.
- A level of belief in a process.

Of those three definitions, the third – a belief in a process – comes closest to what I mean when I refer to ingagement. Yet ingagement is a bigger concept, I like to say that the I stands for Involvement. Ingagement is a process where you involve people to make decisions. From taking part in that process, they become both engaged and ingaged, and believe in the process.

To be clear I'm not referring to a Democratic process where people vote to make decisions. I'm talking more about a process of involvement in which people are able to contribute ideas so that management can make the best decision.

A true ingaged leader does not create phony engagement as a way to manipulate people into being involved. A true ingaged leader genuinely believes that better ideas and processes will develop through active involvement. Ingaged leaders are great leaders because not only do they get the people that work with them to believe and support the initiatives they create, but to create better initiatives through the involvement process.

That is why this book will be about ingagement rather than engagement. Incidentally, I believe in the concept so strongly that I named my company Ingage Consulting. It is not a concept that I take lightly. I strive to live it every day.

How to Use this Book

My goal in writing this book is to present a philosophy and methodology for becoming a leader at a much higher level – an approach that I call ingaged leadership.

It has been my experience that when I discover a book that presents a lot of ideas, it is unlikely that I will use them effectively if I read it from cover to cover and then put it on the shelf. I would therefore like to suggest a few ways to use this book differently.

- **Read the book twice** – If you opt to start at the beginning and read all the way through, I suggest that you then go back and read it for a second time. During that second reading, decide on two or three of the ideas that you would like to put into practice first.

- **Use the book as a focused resource** – Instead of reading the book from start to finish, use the table of contents and the index to locate the sections that can help you with your immediate needs and concerns. If you are about to revamp your approach to conducting employee reviews or hiring the best employees, for example, you can find your way quickly to the ideas to start using immediately.

CHAPTER ONE

What Is Ingagement?

Ingagement is a leadership philosophy for those who believe that it is not enough to tell people what to do, but to involve their minds, creativity and even their emotions. In this chapter, we will get a first glimpse at how ingaged leadership works and how powerful it can be.

What is the philosophy of ingagement? It all starts with a belief that . . .

When you align people and create an organization where everyone works together in partnership, that organization becomes vastly more successful.

Ingagement isn't a single action that you take just once. It is an ongoing, dynamic business practice that has the power to transform your organization, your people, you, and ultimately, your success.

Everyone in a company can create ingagement - company leaders, members of a top leadership team, middle managers and people at many organizational levels. Ingagement goes beyond the kind of management you will find in many companies today, where top executives and middle managers believe that effective leadership means giving instructions or offering incentives.

Ingagement is different. It offers a way of moving from good to great. Ingaged leaders trust people to participate actively in the creation and development of a strategic vision. They openly involve key stakeholders in an ongoing conversation about the organizational vision and how it can be put into action through planning and follow-through.

You develop ingaged leadership when, through your attitude and actions, you let people know that you are partnering with them and that you truly listen.

Authenticity is key to ingagement. When you listen sincerely, you cooperatively create plans and practices which are supported by everyone in your organization, which are much more based in reality, and which become vastly more energized than initiatives that have been developed only by at the top.

To be very clear, ingagement doesn't mean having a democracy. In most organizations, it is the role of senior management and the board to ultimately make the best decisions for an organization in the long term. Yet when people at all levels feel heard, they are more likely to support company plans, even if their own ideas might not have been utilized completely. When people know they have been heard, they are more likely to become invested in their work. They become more eager to continue to share ideas and to cooperate. As a result, the entire organization improves and grows.

What Is Ingagement?

Ingaging Your Key Stakeholders

Ingagement is not limited to internal operations. When successful ingagement extends beyond company walls, it can help you multiply your success. You can achieve that by involving your customers, vendors, distributors, and other stakeholders in open conversation.

From a management perspective, the result is that you build an organization in which more people focus on executing the right things. But getting everyone's priorities and to-do lists directed toward your organization's immediate goals is only part of the picture, because both the power and the reach of ingagement are transformative, not just practical or day-to-day.

To back up those statements, let me tell you the stories of two executives I have known.

EXECUTIVE ONE

Organized, Controlling, Ineffective

I once had the opportunity to closely observe this executive, because I worked in his company. For the purposes of this introduction, let's call him John.

John had a strategic vision for his company. He was actively communicating that vision to everyone in his organization, which was good. However, John also had a non-ingaged philosophy. He was invested in a number of assumptions, common in many executives.

John believed the following assumptions and explained them to me:

- **John thought that people in his company** wanted him to be someone they could "look up to." He believed that it was up to him to set the company strategy, to tell people what it was, and to tell them what they needed to do.

- **John also believed that asking openly for feedback** and ideas would make him a weak leader, because people would believe that he lacked a cohesive, strong vision. He view was that, "If I admit to people that I don't have all the answers, that I could use their help solving problems, they will doubt that I can really lead them."

- **Leadership "style" really counted** for John. He believed that if he focused closely on communicating his vision for the company with energy and conviction, he would motivate people to carry it out. He told me that management should be "So informed, so all-knowing, and so capable that people feel good about following."

So, how successful was John's company? I would be untruthful if I spun a tale in which it failed utterly in the market-

What Is Ingagement?

place. It didn't. It is not that John's leadership style was necessarily bad. The issue is that while his leadership approach was very common, it is far from optimal. I like to wonder how much more successful his organization could have become if he had practiced ingaged leadership, because some very clear operational problems had become ingrained in John's company. Most employees were uninspired and non-supportive. They saw problems but rarely mentioned them, because they felt no one was listening.

Similar problems exist in many organizations today. New and fresh ideas do not circulate freely. Competitors often out-perform them.

Another operational problem? John, just like the many other executives who practice his leadership philosophy, never heard from people in sales, customer service and other front-line positions who could have offered him a wealth of critical intelligence. Any company that finds itself in that position undermines its own competitiveness, alienates employees, and sets a ceiling on its potential for ultimate success.

EXECUTIVE TWO

An Eager but Inauthentic Listener

Let's call our second executive Paul, an executive who saw himself as an enlightened manager. Paul communicated often and attentively with the people in his organization.

When Paul was preparing to attend an intensive leadership workshop, he received a package of pre-workshop materials. Along with the registration forms, there were worksheets to evaluate the effectiveness of Paul's leadership. One of them contained a list of questions for him to distribute to people within his organization.

One question on the worksheet asked Paul's colleagues to evaluate how good a listener he was. Because he had always thought of himself as a good listener, he was expecting to get positive feedback. And positive feedback was exactly what Paul got.

"People replied that I was great at listening to them," Paul recalls. "They also reported that I asked great questions and that when conversations were over, they truly felt that they had been heard. Needless to say, I felt very good about the positive things that people in my organization were saying about my ability to listen."

But then after Paul attended the workshop, his upbeat feelings about his abilities as a listener changed dramatically.

"The workshop showed me that I had never been an honest and open listener," Paul now says. "In fact, I learned that I had been very manipulative. I would ask big, open-ended questions. But inside, I had a negative mindset. I was asking questions only to find out where others were wrong and where I was right. I acted like I was listening, but only to gain people's confidence so that I could uncover their weaknesses. Armed with what they told me, I could prove that they were wrong."

What Is Ingagement?

How do I know so much about this guy named Paul – what was going on in his mind? There's a simple answer. I know those things because I am Paul. (Or maybe more accurately, because I was Paul.) I changed my name when writing this case study, but I am the executive who went to that workshop, which was held at an organization called The Center for Authentic Leadership.

That workshop was the catalyst that inspired me to change the way I listen. I realized that it was time to revise an internal thought process in which I was always searching for areas where other people were wrong. Over time I have been able to convert that process to a new one in which I am always searching for the kernel of truth in what people are saying to me. I had to transition my thought process so that I was not operating from a defensive or adversarial place, but from an inclusive one. As a result, I was able to stop being a negative leader and become one who is dedicated to positive, open and supportive listening.

As my negative outlook and management style started to change, I discovered that I was hearing more great ideas and building on them. Of course there were times when I did not agree completely with someone else's views, priorities, or opinions. Yet my new approach toward listening and communicating created much better results and I became a significantly more effective leader. Now, we were able to discuss, disagree, agree, and explore new possibilities. Through that process, we invariably ended up with results that were far better than we had ever seen before in my organization.

I also came to realize that many executives are impostors when it comes to ingagement, just like I was. Before I began to interact genuinely with people, I was not achieving the success I sought. But through ingagement, the quality of ideas we all generated, including more of my ideas, increased dramatically.

From my experience I learned that people are more likely to support leaders who are willing to receive input without judgment. What a difference!

Concluding thoughts for this chapter . . .

The question is, how do you create ingagement? Ingagement starts with senior management and a true belief that ingagement will lead to a wide range of benefits that include increased employee satisfaction and retention . . . stronger market orientation . . . the ability to adapt more quickly to marketplace trends and events . . . improved customer service and satisfaction . . . and higher efficiency, productivity, and profits.

So how do you get the ball rolling? How do you start your personal and organizational progress toward success through ingagement? We are about to answer those questions in the chapters ahead. I invite you to turn the page, read on, and start the process now.

CHAPTER TWO

Does Ingagement Really Work?

Yes it does.

Here is evidence that will convince you.

If I were you, after reading the last chapter I would be thinking, "It is great that Evan believes so strongly in ingagement and that he feels so positive about it, but where's the proof that it actually works?"

That is a good question to ask. It is one that I have asked myself. I would like to address it in two ways. First, I will provide some statistics from studies that have established the effectiveness of ingagement. Second, I will offer case studies that illustrate how ingagement has produced superlative results.

Research: Gallup Study Shows that Engagement Builds Highly Competitive Companies

Gallup Consulting's "Employee Engagement: What's Your Engagement Ratio" is a landmark study on the benefits of employee engagement within organizations. The study's findings emerged from more than 30 years of research involving more than 17 million employees.

To quote from that study …

> *"The world's top-performing organizations understand that employee engagement is a force that drives business outcomes. Research shows that engaged employees are more productive employees. They are more profitable, more customer-focused, safer, and more likely to withstand temptations to leave the organization. In the best organizations, employee engagement transcends a human resources initiative — it is the way they do business. Employee engagement is a strategic approach supported by tactics for driving improvement and organizational change. The best performing companies know that developing an employee engagement strategy and linking it to the achievement of corporate goals will help them win in the marketplace."*

Gallop created what it calls a "macro-level indicator, called the Engagement Ratio, that serves as a benchmark for the level of employee engagement within organizations. It is a numerical ratio that compares the level of engaged employees to those who are actively disengaged.

Does Ingagement Really Work?

Gallup determined that ratio by asking employees at different companies to respond to the following statements and rate which were true and which were not:

- "I know what is expected of me at work."
- "I have the materials and equipment I need to do my work right."
- "At work, I have the opportunity to do what I do best every day."
- "In the last seven days, I have received recognition or praise for doing good work."
- "My supervisor, or someone at work, seems to care about me as a person."
- "There is someone at work who encourages my development."
- "At work, my opinions seem to count."
- "The mission or purpose of my organization makes me feel my job is important."
- "My associates or fellow employees are committed to doing quality work.
- "I have a best friend at work."
- "In the last six months, someone at work has talked to me about my progress."
- "This last year, I have had opportunities at work to learn and grow."

Based on the responses to those questions, Gallup determined the level of employee engagement in the companies in its study and found that in average-performing organizations, an average of only 33% of employees were engaged, 49% were not engaged, and 18% were actively disengaged. That represented an engagement ratio of 1.83:1, or the ratio of engaged employees to disengaged.

Gallup also determined that in world-class, highly competitive organizations, an average of 67% of employees were engaged; 26% of employees were not engaged; and only 7% were actively disengaged. That represented an engagement ratio of 9.57:1, or the ratio of engaged employees to disengaged.

Gallup concluded that "world-class organizations . . . have an engagement ratio of more than 9:1." And Gallup then went on to make some extraordinary conclusions about the performance of world-class companies (those in the top quartile on its Employee Engagement ratio) when compared to companies that fall in the bottom quartile:

- **Companies with world-class engagement** achieve 3.9 times the earnings per share (EPS) growth.
- **Companies with world-class engagement** exhibit a "dramatic difference" in improved absenteeism, employee retention, workplace safety, customer satisfaction, productivity, and profitability.

Further Research: Data Shows that Ingagement Builds Profits

In a landmark study conducted by Franchise Business Review, 24,050 franchisees representing more than 300 companies were surveyed over a one-year period. One goal was to try to establish a correlation between ingaged communication and organizational success. Another goal was to uncover and understand the key factors that lead to organizational ingagement.

The study employed an analytical tool called the Ingage Barometer, which was developed jointly by my company Ingage Consulting and a research organization called Liminality Inc.

The Ingage Barometer is a sophisticated tool that evaluates levels of ingagement by asking a battery of questions to everyone within an organization. Based on analysis of those responses, organizations are grouped into quartiles. The top quartile encompasses companies that engage in the most inclusive communication. And as you might expect, the companies in the bottom quartile do not.

The results of this study of franchisees concluded that in ingaged organizations:

- **Those in the top quartile** were 3.7 times more likely to report strong financial results than were organizations in the bottom quartile.

- **Those in the top quartile** did much more to promote the success of their brand. In fact, not one of the more than 6000 ingaged organizations in the top quartile stated that they would not recommend their franchise and its system. What about franchisees in the bottom quartile? Forty-seven percent of them stated that they would not actively recommend their franchise to potential new franchisees.

The willingness of franchisees to advocate for their companies is critical, for a very simple reason. When individuals are thinking of buying a franchise, the first thing they do is to call current owners to ask some critical questions about the franchise. Does the parent company communicate effectively with franchise owners? Does it go the extra mile to provide support when and where it is needed?

As you can see, the evidence is quite dramatic that ingagement fuels the success and growth of organizations.

CASE STUDY ONE:
Ingagement Rebuilds a Brand, Supports Profits, and More

Let's move on to some case studies that demonstrate the effectiveness of ingaged leadership. The first is from my own professional life.

Does Ingagement Really Work?

In the year 2000 the company I worked for, CCA Global Partners, acquired our number-one competitor, a company called Flooring America. Prior to our acquisition, Flooring America had 700 locations. About 400 were company-owned, and the rest were owned by franchisees.

But then the Flooring America parent company/franchisor went out of business. The circumstances were troubling, to say the least. Four hundred stores that bore the Flooring America name had going-out-of-business sales. The brand was seriously tarnished.

The owners of those franchises were angry, frustrated, and fearful. They had to go to court to secure various concessions from their former franchisor. And to make it even worse, they also had to deal with the fact that the company that had just acquired them (my company, CCA) had been their main competitor up to that point. Many of those franchisees were in no mood to even speak with people who worked at CCA. Many of them believed that we had only bought Flooring America so that we could close down their businesses and become the dominant player in the flooring industry.

That was not our intention. We made a commitment to bring success to the stores that had been orphaned after Flooring America's failure. And we made good on that commitment, in a very big way. When we took over Flooring America, there were 270 Flooring America locations doing $700 million worth of business. Only four years after we acquired Flooring America, there were close to 600 locations that were doing $2 billion in business a year. In addition, the level of satisfaction among franchisees had soared. Satisfaction actually increased to the highest level among the 15 brands that were part of CCA Global Partners.

How did we overcome resistance, rebuild a damaged brand, more than double sales, and build such high levels of satisfaction?

From day one, it was very clear to me and to my team that if we were to succeed, we would need the support and buy-in of everyone at Flooring America. So we started a program of ingaging everyone. In a very real sense, we needed to have a vision that would both inspire and achieve business results. If we simply tried to inspire people without an effective plan, we would fail. And if we had an effective business plan that didn't inspire people, we would fail too.

We did many things to make our initiative work. We went around the country and held town hall meetings with the Flooring America owners. We wanted them to meet us and share their opinions and ideas. We addressed the most basic questions first. Did they want to retain the Flooring America name, for example, or did they think that the brand had suffered too much damage after the bankruptcy? The owners ultimately decided to keep the name.

We invited owners to rethink how the company sold floor covering. We created a number of advisory councils and did our best to encourage the owners and their staff to participate in them. We also created an umbrella advisory council. Then we extended the council structure and created a marketing council, a training council, a sales council, and more. By building ingagement in those councils, we identified and created leaders within the organization.

We also started regional networking groups called Neighborhood Networks, where individual owners got together on their own to talk about problems and support each other.

Some people in CCA Global worried about what might happen if the Flooring America owners got together independently, with no one from CCA there to watch or take part. But at CCA we decided to trust the owners to meet, discuss, and develop solutions that could help everyone become more successful. In that way, we opened up lines of communication between owners themselves.

In cooperation with the owners and the staff, we built a five-year plan. Everyone contributed and participated in creating it. Through this process a very disgruntled, upset group of individuals bonded, came together and became very passionate. And the organization went from being hyperly dysfunctional to being hyperly functional.

It was a profoundly positive experience. Just to review, we doubled the number of stores in four years and more than doubled the business.

CASE STUDY:
Ingagement Works Its Magic at a Convention

The managers of a leading consumer brand approached me in 2013 with a very specific challenge. Their annual convention was coming up, an event attended by owners of their brand-specific stores across America. The executives were planning to unveil a new store design, and they wanted me to help them increase attendance at the convention.

In previous years, only about 20% of storeowners had come to the convention. And it was a very big priority to get as many of them as possible to attend. Without their buy-in on the new store design, its adoption and use would not be as successful as the company leaders were hoping.

Company leaders were hoping that I could get as many as 40% or 50% of all store owners to come to the convention. But I surpassed that number and was actually able to get more than 85% of them to be there.

How did I help this company achieve those dramatic results? Plain and simple, through ingagement. I began by asking a group of franchisees to describe their experiences at the annual conventions. Most of their comments were similar to this: "I have a lot of fun and everybody socializes, but there is no real reason for me to go. I will never learn anything that company management will not tell me via other means."

Does Ingagement Really Work?

So I went back to management and asked a simple question. Instead of simply pulling the curtains off a new design at the convention, would they consider bringing three or four designs-in-progress and then allowing franchisees to make suggestions about them? Management agreed and showcased several new designs. After franchisees reviewed them, we encouraged them to make suggestions and refinements.

In that way, I was able to shift the dynamic from, "They're going to talk to me" to, "They're going to talk with me." That changed the whole meeting from "95% listen and 5% contribute" to "50% listen and 50% contribute." What a difference.

The result was not only a good design, but also one that reflected the front-line, real-world intelligence that only store-owners could provide. People who provided input were excited about the design that resulted, because they had enjoyed a role in creating it. I predict that as stores roll out the new design, their customers are going to love it – and that profits will increase.

Snapshots of Ingagement at Work

An ingaged leadership approach is winning acceptance in more and more businesses today. Even in organization where the term "ingagement" is not used, company leaders are noticing that operations simply run better when employees' contributions are heard, utilized and rewarded. Profits grow, employee retention improves, products are better aligned with customers' needs and desires, and other positive benefits increase.

Here are some short case studies of organizations where that is taking place today.

- **At Enterasys Networks,** a division of Siemens, company leaders are achieving remarkable success from some very simple ways to increase employee ingagement. Executives and employees at every level through the organization are encouraged to ask each other the question "What do you think?" at least once a day. Executives are also encouraged not only to implement an "open door" policy, but to actually remove the doors from their office entrances. Vala Afshar, Chief Marketing Office and Chief Customer Officer for Enterasys Networks, writes on the SAP Business Innovation blog, "We have had incredible success with more than three years of consecutive topline revenue growth. We have also received numerous industry awards for our innovative products and services."

- **At REI recreational outfitters,** company leaders have created a series of "company campfire" events, hosted on social media, where employees can share ideas, stories and suggestions. About 50% of all REI employees take part, which could account for the chain's strong growth in the marketplace. According to data on the

Does Ingagement Really Work?

company website, annual sales exceeded $2.0 billion in 2013, an increase of 5.9 percent from $1.9 billion the previous year.

- At Cummins, the maker of engines and industrial equipment, all employees are encouraged to take part side-by-side in community service projects. According to Cummins, the informal connections and interactions that take place in those settings have contributed to 2014 revenues of $19.2 billion (up from $1.65 billion in 2013) and a Fortune 500 ranking of 186 in 2013.

- When I was working at CCA Global Partners in Manchester New Hampshire, CEO Howard Brodsky was using a simple, yet highly effective program to build ingagement through the ranks of his organization. Each month he held a lunch meeting for seven or eight employees, always at a local restaurant. The meetings were not exclusively for middle managers or executives. Anyone could attend. "I didn't want to give the lunches a formal name," he explains, "because I wanted to keep everything somewhat loose." Yet Deb Binder, a former CCA employee who was working there at the times, recalls that "If you got an invitation to go to lunch with the CEO, that was pretty exciting." If people who had not been invited wanted to attend, they were welcome to do that. Everyone could ask anything that they wanted, and no professional or personal topic was off-limits. Practical new ideas emerged from those meetings, but the greatest benefit was that people understood that they were valued. Their ideas would be heard, and often tested or used, by an organization that wanted to hear what they had to say.

- **When I was President at Carpet One,** we took our entire staff on a retreat once a year. We did team-building exercises in the mornings. In the afternoons, we invited all the employees to attend open meetings that were held in a big room outfitted with nothing but chairs and flipcharts. Senior management (comprised of me and the people who reported directly to me) did not attend. All the attendees were invited to walk up to a flipchart, write down any topic they pleased, and start a discussion about it. In essence, we were giving people a forum where they could discuss anything without worrying about upsetting anybody from upper management, or getting judged. As the meetings progressed, people were able to go up to the flipcharts, review the topics that were under discussion, and offer new ideas. An extraordinary number of great ideas emerged – ideas about HR, customer service and relationships, operational efficiency, and a lot more. When the retreats ended, we had people put the very best ideas on big pieces of paper from the flip charts. When we went back to our home office, we posted those big sheets on the wall, got working on them, and posted progress. People could see that their best ideas were not only heard, but put into practice. As a result, they felt motivated to suggest even more ideas. It was a real benefit to both the employees and to the organization.

- When I was at CCA, we created a series of monthly team meetings called ECHO ("Everyone Collaborates and Helps the Organization") meetings. They were unusual meetings, because the participants were from three different companies that were all involved in different aspects of the floor covering business. We created sub-groups by function – such as marketing, merchandising and distribution – and had meetings where members of each of those groups could meet their counterparts from the other companies. People were encouraged to discuss challenges that they were facing, to share solutions, and more. A number of great ideas were generated and participants discovered many new ways to cooperate, save money, and become more efficient. The participating companies realized, for example, that they could save money by using the same printer to produce their brochures. They discovered that if they shipped their displays at the same time with the same trucking company, they would save even more by negotiating lower shipping costs. Then the ECHO participants dug a little deeper internally, and found new ways to use their ideas to benefit as many different divisions of their companies as possible. All three companies benefitted because they were able to share ideas freely. They were saving money, boosting profits, generating new ideas, and building a lot of ingagement and excitement through their ranks. It was a huge success.

- **At Carpet One,** we launched a program of 12 Town Hall meetings. First, we invited all our 780 members to contribute their ideas for our new strategic plan. We then held meetings with our Advisory Council, where those ideas were developed. We next hosted 12 more Town Hall meetings and presented the plan. The result was a very strong and motivational plan that we used to create an infographic that was distributed to every location, to be shared with all employees.

- **Dean Marcarelli, CCA Global Partners' Chief Marketing Officer,** used to hold off-site marketing meetings with the marketing staffs of all of CCA's 12 companies. People would share ideas and work on joint problems. Marketing experts were brought in to educate and stimulate new ideas for the company. From time to time Dean would invite marketing executives from companies outside of CCA to join to add fresh perspectives to the meetings. Everyone learned, shared ideas, and cooperated. It is just one more example of the transformational force of ingaged leadership.

Do You Have to Become an Ingaged Leader?

Can't You Practice Other Leadership Styles and Still Be Successful?

It is important to ask that question. My honest answer is that no, you are not required to master the art of ingaged leadership if you do not want to. But it is an option that is available to you, and one that I think merits your serious consideration.

There have been leaders in different fields – company leaders, elected officials, generals, sports coaches – who have used a top-down, directive approach instead. Some of them have achieved notable things, even without seeking to ingage the hearts and minds of the people in their organizations. I am not saying that those people are wrong, or that I am right. I am simply offering a different approach to leading on what I think is a higher level – one that has worked for me, one that might work beautifully for you, and one that promises remarkable results in many of today's organizations where teamwork, personal involvement and shared vision have brought success.

You don't have to adopt and apply every idea in this book. But if the philosophy of ingaged leadership makes sense to you, and if you find the approach worth testing, I believe that this book will help you discover new ways to achieve extraordinary things.

Concluding thoughts for this chapter...

Good things happen when you talk with people instead of talking at them. And of course, when you really listen. Great things happen when you tap into the power of ingagement.

CHAPTER THREE

Practical Ways to Master the Art of Ingaged Management

Ingagement, like any practical leadership philosophy, needs to be put into practice every day in a variety of situations and contexts. To do that, you need a toolbox of skills that you can apply when necessary. In this chapter, we will explore the most important tools that you should have at the ready as you lead from day to day.

The ingaged organization you will build can be like a beautiful, fast, and responsive automobile. It will be capable of taking you anywhere, quickly. But because you will be the driver at the controls, you have some decisions to make. How and where will you steer the car? Who will give you directions? When should you speed up and when should you slow down? When will your beautiful automobile need repairs, a rebuild, or just a simple tune-up so that it can continue to operate smoothly and efficiently?

I know that is just an analogy, and analogies tend to be flawed. But even so, let's explore some practical concepts that can help you lead your organization to the right destinations and achieve beautiful results.

Define and Address the Causes of Problems, Not the Symptoms

If you are trying to solve a problem in your organization, here is an important question to ask...

Are you addressing the symptoms of the problem, or the cause?

Let's say, for example, that your salespeople are not meeting your expectations or sales quotas. In many organizations, leaders will define the problem in just that way, saying, "Our salespeople are bad at selling, that's the problem."

Yet if those company leaders dug deeper, they could identify root causes of the problem that, if addressed, could lead to more effective solutions. The root problems could be issues like these:

- We do not have the right products to compete in the marketplace.

- We do not have the right pricing.

- We have supply or delivery problems that cause our customers to buy from our competitors.

- Our customer service is not good enough to motivate first-time buyers to become repeat customers.

Practical Ways to Master the Art of Ingaged Management

- We have a training or coaching problem.
- We are not taking steps to be sure that we hire the right salespeople.
- We are not equipping our salespeople with the right tools.

> **ACTION STEP**
>
> Think of an issue that you are facing in your company – a problem that you are trying to solve. Try to dig deeper and deeper down until you have identified all the possible root causes of it. Then decide which of them to address first, and how. Remember that other people will be able to offer you a wider range perspectives and suggestions than you can generate if you attempt to define or solve the problem on your own.

To pinpoint the root cause of the problem, you can ask questions like these:

- "Why do you think we have a sales problem?"
- "What are our most successful salespeople doing to sell this product?"

- "What are those successful salespeople not doing?"
- "Are there any marketing issues related to this problem?"
- "Are there any competitor issues?"

Again, you need to keep digging down to the root cause. You also need to talk to all the people involved – people from the sales team, the marketing team, and other appropriate personnel – to get at the underlying issues. Be sure to talk with customers and potential customers too.

Tap the Power of Collaboration

Leaders at many companies typically use the term collaboration to describe brainstorming sessions that are held to generate ideas around a specific topic or problem. The leaders of those companies often seem to believe that effective collaboration means getting people together into the same room to air big ideas.

I see the power of collaboration as being so much more. It goes beyond generating ideas and gives people a sense of ownership. When people genuinely collaborate, they become invested in the success of current processes and the overall success of your organization, too.

Even if you are extremely astute in business and know what needs to be done to succeed, I encourage you to still involve your team in finding solutions.

Practical Ways to Master the Art of Ingaged Management

If you go to your team and say, "Here are the answers to our current challenge . . . here is what I want us to do," their initial reaction will be to evaluate what they're being told. It's just human nature. They will ask themselves questions like, "Do I like his idea . . . how does it impact me . . . is it really a good idea . . . isn't there a better answer or solution?"

You will discover that you can achieve far better results if you bring people together and say, "We need to work together on this issue. I have some ideas, and I'm sure you have ideas, too. What do we need to do?" If you spend time thinking about it and discussing it as a group – and if you are open to letting people make improvements to your best ideas – the end result will be a group of people working together to make the best solutions happen.

So collaboration isn't just about making better ideas. It's about building ingagement and effectiveness to make great things happen.

CASE STUDY

A Salesman Grows

Those are demonstrable benefits of collaboration yet nonetheless, many executives don't take the time to collaborate. Instead, they fall back on the traditional management style of, "If I ask people to do something, they should just do it."

My family's business was a classic example. We had a salesperson who was phenomenal. He typically outsold all the other salespeople in the company. And when he would request simple and basic favors from the people he worked with, such as things he needed for his customers, he was typically met with resistance. That was because he didn't take time to tell people why he needed what he was requesting. He didn't ask for opinions - he wouldn't collaborate at all. As a result, the other employees became resentful and weren't eager to do what he asked, and he couldn't understand why. When I explained why he encountered such resistance (and by now all you readers should all understand that it had something to do with his lack of ingagement), his response was, "Well, I'm the top salesperson so if I just say to do it, that should be good enough."

His authoritarian attitude started to negatively affect his business. At a certain point he realized in order to continue selling successfully, he needed to adjust.

He started taking the time to involve the other employees by saying, "I have an issue with a client . . . Here is what is going on . . . I need some help . . . Do you have any suggestions? . . . Have you tried something that has worked better?" The other members of the team became supportive. And if they had a better idea, they had an opportunity to share it.

In time, he grew and ended up closing 10 times more sales than the average salesperson did. Through ingagement, he built success through the support of his company team and his customer team too.

Remember that "Just because I said so" Is not Good Enough

If you are a company leader or a manager who supervises a staff, the reality is that "just because I asked" isn't good enough. In the short term you can bully or intimidate people, but for the durable health and success of your organization, you need to take steps like these toward fuller collaboration:

- **Explain** why you want something done.
- **Ask** people for their opinions.
- **Strive** to approach challenges in better and different ways.

You should not take these steps because they make people feel better, but because they lead to better outcomes.

ACTION STEP

Reflect on how you talk to people and request their ideas and help. Do you take the time to explain the issue you are facing? Do you check to ensure that they understand why you are asking? Do you leave an opening for them to suggest better ideas and solutions?

Get in the Habit of Asking for Help

Very few people like to ask for help. It's a personality thing. Some people are just too shy to ask. Others hesitate to ask because they feel they are bothering or inconveniencing other people. Still others feel that if they ask for help, they will appear incapable, unintelligent or unresourceful.

I have a totally different take on this issue, based on my experience. I am convinced other people feel validated and appreciated when I ask them for help. I also believe that people typically enjoy giving help, because we all naturally feel good about helping others. Another benefit is that when someone helps you, they sense that you "owe" them a favor in return. That can establish a pattern of healthy cooperation and give-and-take.

I often say to people, "Please ask me for help if you ever need anything." Even if I don't say that, people know they can ask me, because I have established a pattern of being helpful. And I think those efforts have helped build deeper relationships and greater organizational success.

I'm not suggesting you ask for help just for the sake of asking for help, or just to make people feel good. When you do need help, however, don't shy away from asking. People will appreciate you more. When you ask people for assistance, you demonstrate that you respect their expertise and effort. That will help create a stronger bond between you and those around you.

An added benefit? Asking for help tells someone that you know you're not perfect. It shows a more human side to you as a leader. It's not a weakness, it's a strength, because you show that you are strong enough to know you need to ask for help. Asking for help is a sign that you're a confident person, not an arrogant one.

> **ACTION STEP**
>
> Over the next few days, consciously take time to ask people for more help. Consider their reactions. Over time, evaluate how your relationships with those people have improved.

Focus on Key Performance Indicators

There is so much power in the simple process of identifying and monitoring performance indicators. When you do that, you become involved in what your employees focus on and what they need to achieve. And when they do achieve the levels of improvement you have set as goals, your people will also have the ability to congratulate themselves on success.

Ultimately, when you do those things, the bottom line that you care about — your net profits — will improve as a result. Profit is not a Key Performance Indicator, it is a result.

Key Performance Indicators are measures of the activities that will improve your profitability if you handle them well. They could be as simple as the number of new customers you acquire in every quarter or every year, your inventory levels, or your in-stock levels.

Sample Key Performance Indicators

Here are some performance indicators that you might decide to monitor:

- Average sale size
- Customer satisfaction rates or Net Promoter Score
- Days from order to delivery
- Employee ingagement levels
- The closing rates of sales
- The cost of goods sold
- The number of new sales leads that you are generating
- The number of sales per employee
- Website traffic

Practical Ways to Master the Art of Ingaged Management

Take Time to Frame How You See Things

I love to ski. I actually love skiing through groves of trees. The trick to successfully skiing in the trees is not to look at the trees, but at the path between them.

The same is true about business. It is best to think about what you need to do to be successful, not what you need to avoid.

If you think about what you need to avoid while skiing - i.e. the trees - you are far more likely to hit the trees. People are naturally drawn to what they think about. For better outcomes, focus your attention instead on what needs to be done to be successful, not on problems to avoid.

Often, it's as simple as saying things differently:

- Ask, "Where can we find new areas to operate with greater efficiency?" instead of, "We need to cut costs."
- Or ask, "What do we need to learn about our customers' most pressing concerns?" rather than, "We can't lose any more customers."

Framing things positively can have a huge impact on you, everyone around you, and your ultimate success.

Take Time to Get Fresh Perspective

It is so easy for us to get caught up in the day-to-day process of running and managing our businesses that we lose perspective. And when we do, we fall into the trap of doing things the way we always have. I like to think about it this way . . .

> *The higher up you are in your organization, the greater the percentage of time becomes that you should spend working <u>on</u> your business, not working <u>in</u> your business.*

A functional manager, someone who manages a call center for example, can perhaps spend 95% of the day supervising subordinates, tracking calling activity, and handling the other day-to-day requirements of the job. That would leave 5% of the day to reflect on how to do the job, make improvements, etc. But if you are a CEO, you should spend 95% of your time reflecting on your business, considering what is happening in other industries, talking to senior executives at other companies, talking to your customers and senior executives and performing higher-level activities. If you are a middle manager, depending on the nature of your responsibilities, you might be able to invest 10% of your time reflecting on bigger issues and 90% of your time performing your job. The higher you are up on the company hierarchy, the more time you should spend working on, not in.

There are many ways to discover fresh perspectives. Regularly explore the marketplace – physically and through magazines, journals and online. The concepts that you discover can be game changing.

Traveling to other countries can also open your eyes to new approaches. When I was in the floor covering business, for example, I got many ideas when I travelled to Europe. I saw that stores there did things quite differently from the way we did in the U.S. I found ideas that had validity back home.

Another important activity is to look at competition not just in your space, but at companies in other industries that are courting the customers that you are. You are selling products that require those customers to spend dollars, but those customers also have the choice to spend their money in other ways. So if you look closely at what companies are doing in other industries and sectors, you can develop new ideas about how you can compete for those dollars.

Ask for Input

Truly strong leaders are always asking questions and learning. They are not arrogant or autocratic.

Asking for input is a bit different from asking for help. When you ask for input, you are not asking for one-time assistance with a particular challenge. You are soliciting a wider range of ideas and suggestions on larger issues and topics.

Nothing is more critical than getting others involved in the larger processes that you are working on. There are many settings in which you can ask for input, including town-hall style meetings, strategic planning sessions, councils that convene periodically, surveys, and more.

When you actively invite input, some very positive things happen. People will:

- Develop a vested interest in your success
- See your request as a sign that you are confident in yourself and open to new ideas
- Become advocates and ongoing contributors, not occasional acquaintances
- Become vested in your successful outcomes
- Be more motivated to improve the quality of the ideas they suggest to you

When you ask people for input, they become more motivated to do whatever it takes to make sure you are successful. You can reap all those benefits, just by asking for input.

Practical Ways to Master the Art of Ingaged Management

Fight Complacency

("Business is good so I don't need to improve it")

Complacency comes in a variety of forms. You can recognize it in statements like these:

- "Business is good – I'd like it to keep going well, so I don't need to do anything."
- "If it ain't broke, don't fix it."
- "I'm making enough money, I don't need to make more."

I actually had someone tell me, "I don't need to raise my margins. I'm making enough money. I'd rather just give more to my customers." On the surface that sounds noble, but it isn't. Profits might seem like greed, but they're not. They're really about growing and investing in your business. They're about protecting your job and your employees' jobs. Every business needs profits.

So if you're suffering from this pitfall and believe your business is so good that you don't need to grow it, I urge you to shake things up a bit.

Unfortunately, your competitors probably didn't get that same message that they are doing well enough. They are innovating and growing their businesses. That is one reason why you constantly have to make your business better.

Another temptation to become complacent . . .

Some people seem to believe that if they work harder, they will destroy their work-life balance. Now, I am a very big believer in establishing a good work-life balance. But the reality is that you want your business to achieve all it can achieve. And I like to remember that even in a company that has become wildly successful, it is still possible for people to enjoy time with their families.

To summarize, work-life balance doesn't mean your business goes on hold so you can attend to personal pursuits. The reality is if your business is on hold, your business is going backwards. Some other company is going to outperform you. You will then have a serious issue when your business is going to go bad. And leading an enterprise that is going downhill will have a way of doing more harm to your work-life balance than you believed possible.

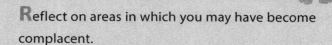

ACTION STEP

Reflect on areas in which you may have become complacent.

Practical Ways to Master the Art of Ingaged Management

Decide How Much Collaboration to Encourage, and When

As a leader, part of your job is to decide the level of collaboration that you will encourage in different circumstances:

- Large-scale collaboration - There are times when it makes sense to involve everyone in your organization to weigh in and collaborate. If you are making a new commitment to improving the ratings you are receiving for your customer service, for example, you will probably want to gather insights from your customer service representatives, salespeople, call center personnel, the dealers who sell your products, other people who are in contact with customers, and customers.

- Collaboration with specific internal teams - There are also times when you should decide to collaborate and get input from a limited number of people in your organization, such as the members of your top executive team, your sales managers, your IT and tech people, or other groups that possess the specific knowledge and experience that equip them to give insights into the process or change that you are considering.

- Collaboration with specific external teams - There can also be times when you want input and help from people outside your internal organization, such as groups of customers, dealers or franchisees. Part of your job as a leader is to understand and invite the right people into different processes.

After gathering insights and information, there can also come a time when you, if you are the executive leader, make an autonomous decision to move ahead with something. Most companies, after all, do not function like democracies where everyone gets to vote on all big-picture issues. There sometimes comes a time when individuals who are practicing the art of leadership need to make considered decisions to move ahead.

> **ACTION STEP**
>
> Review how you have collaborated on specific tasks and projects in the past. Did you involve the right people? If you could attack the same issue or challenge again, would you invite the same people to collaborate with you? If not, whom would you invite instead?

Practical Ways to Master the Art of Ingaged Management

Build Ingagement through Participation

We often hear people say, "If we did everything by committee, we'd never get anything done." While there may be some truth to that, consider this statement: "If we never got input from people, think of all the mistakes we would make."

Genuine participation in important projects and processes is one of the keys to success. Encouraging people to participate and plan projects (especially those that affect them directly) can help improve the level of ingagement within any organization. Here are some steps you can take to encourage participation:

- **Consider everyone to be a stakeholder** - Talk to people, ask them how they would address problems, listen to them, and strive to understand the issue from their perspective. Remember, the more involved they are in a project, the more they will be invested in its success.

- **Use task forces and ideas committees to promote innovation** – Create steering committees of thought leaders within your organization to get input, insight and commitment. Encourage people to ask, "How does this initiative help us get us closer to achieving our organization's goals?" and, "How does it align with our mission, vision and values?"

- **Look for opportunities for managers and employees to participate in the communication process** – Encourage them to contribute articles and other resources, invite feedback on the information they have provided, share information, conduct polls and to be proactive in communications within your organization.

Have the Courage to Allow People to Take Risks

I believe it is important to let people take risks. Sometimes, those risks can even carry the possibility of failure.

I know that sounds counterintuitive, and you are probably asking, "Are you really suggesting that if I know that one of my managers is going to do something wrong, I should let that person go ahead and fail? Why does that make any sense at all?

Yet I believe that it often does make sense to allow people to try things that you do not agree with, or that you have seen fail in the past. Yet allow me to inject a note of caution here. As a leader, your job is to assess the risk in different situations and make a decision about where and when to apply the philosophy of letting people try risky things. You would not allow your managers to fail in extremely important activities

Practical Ways to Master the Art of Ingaged Management

where the consequences of failure would be too great.

Nonetheless, here are several compelling reasons for allowing your managers to take risks:

- First, if you always protect people from making mistakes, they will never develop the confidence to do anything on their own. They will never have the gumption to try brave new things, take risks, innovate, or accomplish results that are truly exceptional.

- Second, you reduce the risk of becoming a micromanager. When people have the autonomy to move ahead, they will not need to ask your permission to execute every small assignment that lies ahead of them. As a result, you will be able to let go of lower-level activities that should no longer occupy the time and attention of a higher-level executive.

- Third, you will never learn that some of your opinions could be wrong. Opinions, we know, tend to be flawed. Do you really know that all of yours are valid? Have you taken time to validate and research them? Have changes occurred in the world that you have not considered – changes that could make your opinions out-of-date? If you allow people to move ahead even though you recognize a risk of failure, you will be amazed at how many times they will surprise you by succeeding. One example? A marketing person approaches you and says that he intends to run an advertisement in a particular publication and you want to say, "I ran an ad there five years ago, and it failed miserably. Don't do it." But if you have the courage to let him run that ad, you might just learn that changes have occurred that will cause that advertisement to succeed. Perhaps your products or services now have a more competitive advantage in the marketplace. Perhaps the readership of the publication has changed and more of your targeted customers are reading it today. Perhaps your product has become the only one of its kind that is produced domestically, and potential customers are eager to buy products that are made in America.

The bottom line is that when you ride in and prevent people from taking actions that you believe are risky, you eliminate the possibility that they will bring something new and better to your enterprise. They might have a new twist on an old idea. They might try something in a slightly different way. If you prevent them from trying, you only prevent them from finding some new kind of success.

Cultivate Positive Reflection, not "Yes People"

The term "Yes Person" describes someone who says yes to everything, who always agrees with you. If you are in a position of power and you're not actively seeking ingaged collaboration from your staff and team, there is a very real risk that your people will become "Yes People." They will sometimes knowingly follow a directive that will harm the company instead of pushing back and asking questions. That road clearly leads to reduced effectiveness and even failure. You want to develop a team that will contribute to find better outcomes.

If you don't feel your staff contributes a lot of ideas or asks questions when they're asked to execute something, then you are most likely creating "Yes People." Asking for opinions does take more time, but the investment you make will result in better ideas. Plus, your employees will be more supportive in making important things happen.

Take Time to Cultivate Repeat and Referral Business

There's a saying that says, "Your next most likely customer is your last customer."

That statement is normally true. But there is more to it than that, because your current best customers offer you the best opportunities to grow your business. You can do more business with them, and they can refer new customers to you.

If you are not devoting enough attention to cultivating repeat and referral business, you are limiting your opportunities to grow. Some steps to take:

- **Identify your key top customers.** To find out who they are, be sure to speak with your salespeople, customer service representatives and other people on the front lines.
- **Start an ongoing conversation with them.** Ask how you can improve your business with them.
- **Ask them if they can introduce you to businesses that would benefit from working with you or buying from you.** In most cases, they will be happy to do so.

I think you'll be surprised and delighted to see how happy your customers will be to help you grow your business. Customers like to help. Also, they know that if they refer new customers to you, you will be motivated to return the favor by being more helpful to them.

It all starts by simply pinpointing who your best customers are and then starting a conversation with them.

Practical Ways to Master the Art of Ingaged Management

Keep Lines of Communication Open with Your Vendors

It's extremely tempting to look at a vendor as little more than someone who sells you stuff. If you can change that mindset and see vendors as partners, they can become a great source of information and knowledge that can support your efforts to build ingagement.

It all starts with soliciting ideas and input from vendors, but you might not want to work in that way with all of your vendors. It pays to consider all your vendors and invite those who will be most likely to bring good things to a closer collaboration. One good approach is to resolve to work more closely with vendors with whom you already have deep, positive relationships.

Like your customers, your vendors can offer you important insights, including:

- **Front-line information** about trends, news and technology in your industry

- **Objective opinions** about what your organization is doing and what it needs to do

- **Important intelligence** about how people see your company in comparison to your competitors – and maybe even some important intelligence about what those competitors are planning and doing

Gaining all those benefits starts by simply asking vendors to offer you input and advice.

Cultivate the Ability to "Eat Elephants"

You have probably heard the old question, "How do you eat an elephant?" The answer to it is, "One bite at a time."

I believe the answer to that question is a good one to keep in mind every day as a leader and a manager. Instead of feeling overwhelmed by the enormity of certain critical initiatives or processes that you would like to tackle, simply get started by taking a small step – in effect, by "taking one small bite."

You know what those big elephants are – they are the projects that seem so complex that you tend to put them off. One could be writing a business plan for a new company or division that you would like to launch, so that you can obtain funding. Another might be studying the efficiencies of the outsourced call centers you are using so that you can decide whether or not to open an internal call center of your own.

When we are faced with tasks like those, "taking a first bite" is critically important. That bite could be creating an internal task force to explore an issue or calling some of your contacts to ask for input.

The first bite can be small. But here's one piece of advice that I can offer. Whatever that first bite will be, try to take it soon. Do it today, if at all possible.

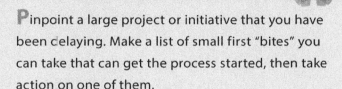

ACTION STEP

Pinpoint a large project or initiative that you have been delaying. Make a list of small first "bites" you can take that can get the process started, then take action on one of them.

Concluding thoughts for this chapter...

As you have read this chapter, did any of its concepts "speak" to you? Did any of them strike you as areas where you could improve, or as areas that would offer significant returns if you addressed them? Chances are that some of them did. If that is the case, I'd encourage you to focus on them in the days and weeks ahead. As you have noticed in your work and career, people who continuously work to improve themselves, their teams and their organizations become highly effective leaders.

CHAPTER FOUR

Understanding and Communicating Your Company's Identity and Purpose

Every organization has a purpose and stands for something. Whether you're an executive or a manager, your ability to lead becomes vastly more effective when you understand just what that purpose is and use it to ingage and inspire those around you. In this chapter, we will explore ways to understand what that purpose is and to use it more effectively in your leadership.

Sometimes the seeds of a company's identity were sown by the founder, or by a group of individuals who started the organization. But no identity is static and over time, it evolves as it affected by new company leaders, employees, new company initiatives, trends in the marketplace and even by competitors.

No matter how your organization has evolved, your ability to be an ingaged leader relies on your willingness to understand and define who you are, and then to communicate that identity to people inside and outside your organization.

So who are you? That knowledge comes from considering questions like these:

- What do we stand for?
- Where have we been?
- Where are we going?
- What makes us unique?

- How are we perceived as a company?
- What is it about our company that makes people want to work here and build their future with us?

Let's dig a bit deeper by considering some of the traits of positive and negative company cultures.

Organizations with positive company cultures often . . .

- Have a high level of ethics
- Are committed to community, environmental and other values (i.e., a sustainability mindset)
- Enjoy an atmosphere of teamwork and camaraderie
- Have a shared sense of community
- Encourage creativity and thrive on innovation
- Promote risk-taking
- Are customer-focused
- Keep employees' families in mind and promote a positive work/life balance
- Foster a positive approach and sense of fun
- Provide generous benefits
- Encourage employees' personal and professional development
- Embrace continuous learning

- Create opportunities for growth and advancement
- Have strong and shared core values
- Promote technological innovation
- Are fiscally realistic

Walk into a company with a positive culture and you will see happy, relaxed people working hard and without tension. You'll hear people who are sharing ideas, consulting each other, and laughing. There is a sense of openness. You will feel relaxed and welcomed.

Organizations with negative company cultures often . . .

- Maintain false communication where everyone "weighs in," yet few feel heard and results are delayed
- Neglect collaboration
- Ignore unhealthy and, in some cases illegal, behavior such as sexism, male dominance, racism, intolerance, emotional and physical abuse
- Disregard disruptive internal competition and sniping
- Suffer from minimal employee loyalty
- Lose time and money to low productivity and high turnover
- Have unnecessary hierarchies

- Lack a healthy life/work balance
- Tend to be rigid and continue to "do it the way we've always done it"

When you visit a company with a poor corporate culture, you will feel tension that permeates every level. You will see grim faces. You will likely notice many offices with closed doors. You may feel uncomfortable, without knowing why. The reason is that everyone who works there is uncomfortable and disconnected.

> **ACTION STEP**
>
> Take some time and review the factors that create company culture. Where does your current company culture belong among the categories that we mentioned above? Where would you like it to be? What changes will you make to get there?

It Takes Positive People to Create a Positive Culture

We will explore the issue of staffing in depth in Chapter Seven. At this point in this book, let me simply observe that as you clarify your vision for what you want your culture to become over time, it will become clearer to you whether you have the right people on board to support that culture. And you might come to some surprising conclusions. I know one organization, for example, that had to come face-to-face with the realization that some of its more profit-producing staff members, and also the most valued, were individuals who did not like to share ideas openly with other people. Yet even if you discover something troubling like that about your staffing, over time you can build toward the culture you want through transformative activities like:

- **Hiring.** Recruit people who possess the traits and outlooks that support the culture that you want to build. Once you define the culture you want to create and start building it, more of the right people will discover you and want to work for you.

- **Compartmentalizing.** Remember that it is generally not necessary for every employee to embody everything that you want your culture to be. If a manufacturer is developing a culture of creativity, for example, it might be more critical to encourage that trait in product designers and marketers than in product assemblers. Yet you do want to have people in key leadership and management positions who are committed to the values you want to achieve.

- **Coaching and training.** Some people find it very difficult to change less-than-ideal behaviors that have proved to be successful. Yet as a leader or influential manager, you have more ability to influence people than you might expect.

Be Forward-Thinking and Envision What You Want to Become

It is sometimes worthwhile to ask, "So what did we do in the past that worked? Why don't we bring it back?" Sometimes that approach works, but always reaching back to what worked in the past is generally not growthful. After all, future trends and changes will influence who you become as an organization.

Few leaders – even excellent ones – have the ability to predict the future with complete accuracy. However, questions like these will help you get a vision of how you will evolve in the years ahead:

- **How have our customers changed** and what does that tell me about how they could change in the future?
- **Are there technological changes** that we will have to adopt in order to thrive?

- What is the projected life of our offerings – are they still competitive, at what point will we need to discontinue them, alter them, or upgrade them in order to stay competitive?

- How might our competitors fare in the years ahead – are they growing stronger or weaker? What are their key competitive advantages and disadvantages against us?

ACTION STEP

Reflect on the business you are in and make a list of predictions about the changes that are about to happen in your industry in the next five years.

Practical Ways to Define Who You Are ... So You Can Communicate Your Culture and Plans More Effectively

I recommend creating several working documents that help you understand and communicate where you are and where you are going as an organization.

Create a Mission Statement

A mission statement is a short, succinct statement that tells

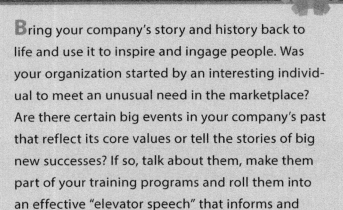

ACTION STEP

Bring your company's story and history back to life and use it to inspire and ingage people. Was your organization started by an interesting individual to meet an unusual need in the marketplace? Are there certain big events in your company's past that reflect its core values or tell the stories of big new successes? If so, talk about them, make them part of your training programs and roll them into an effective "elevator speech" that informs and inspires.

all your stakeholders – your leadership team, your employees, your customers and the world – who you are and what you do. In the case of my consulting company, our mission is "We are ingagement champions. We help our clients succeed by helping them build strong, ingaged organizations."

Create a Vision Statement Too

A vision statement is different from a mission statement because it describes what you want your organization to become in a larger sense. In our case, we want to be the world's most widely recognized and respected thought leaders in the field of ingaged leadership and management.

As you consider the vision for your organization and de-

Understanding and Communicating Your Company's Identity and Purpose

cide how to communicate it, it can be a good idea to benchmark against renowned individuals and companies with strong and compelling visions. For example, Tom Peters immediately comes to mind when someone mentions business excellence, thanks to his 1982 book In Search of Excellence. And Stephen R. Covey is top-of-mind when the philosophy of effective leadership is mentioned. He came to national attention in 1989 with the publication of his first book, The 7 Habits of Highly Effective People.

What will you and your organization become? What are your biggest hopes and aspirations? They should form the core of your vision statement.

Do ingage other people in the process of defining and refining your vision.

That can mean resisting the temptation to develop it in the vacuum of a senior management meeting.

CASE STUDY

How Chipotle Defines its Mission and Vision

Chipotle, one of the hottest restaurant chains on the American landscape today, frames its mission and vision this way:

- Chipotle's mission (what the company does) is to *"serve food with integrity."*

- **Chipotle's vision** (its aspiration for what it will become) is to "*change the way people think about fast food.*"

Communicate Who You Are in a Strategic Way

I recommend that you communicate your mission, vision statement and strategic plan purposefully.

What do I mean by purposefully? I mean sharing your planning documents with your employees and probably also with key customers and suppliers, provided they play a large and significant role in your success. You might also want to share certain parts of your plan on your website – but probably not your full long-range plan.

Some people will question the wisdom of sharing internal documents too freely. They wonder how wise it is to let your competitors see so much information about your company and your plans. I understand and respect that argument. But at the same time, how can you go somewhere when your team doesn't know where you are going, your vendors don't know, and your customers don't know? If that is the case, you are wandering.

In my experience, it would be highly unlikely for a competitor to steal your plans and use them more successfully than you can. Your competitors, after all, have their own plans, agendas, and challenges to address. They are only as effective as their ability to execute their own plans. Just because they can see your mission, vision and plan doesn't mean they can execute them.

Refine Your Vision through Long-Term Planning

It is crucial to push yourself to think long term, not short term. That might sound like a complex and difficult process, but you can get started by asking some fundamental questions:

- **If I were starting fresh** and wanted to start an enterprise that would put my own organization out of business, what would I do?
- **If I were starting again** and wanted to open a business that would put everyone else out of business, what would I do?

Those questions will help you identify some of the critical things you should be doing, and eliminate the minutiae that are probably claiming most of your time now. Make a list of the biggest and most ambitious issues you are facing. Then determine if it is possible to solve them – and when, and how. They can help you create a vision for your company and identify specific challenges and tasks that can help you grow into a much more successful organization.

Ingaging Leadership

Let Your Customers Help Define Who You Are

It's important that you understand what your customers do and how what you do affects them. You will then be a better partner to them. You will also:

- Gain valuable end-user generated, real-world insights
- Avoid developing tunnel vision and groupthink
- Stay grounded, because customers tell you things about your organization that are very hard to learn anywhere else

You can connect directly with individuals from a cross-section of your customer base, or invite them to working meetings. Stress that their assistance will strengthen your relationship and lead to shared benefits. Including customers in this process is always productive.

CASE STUDY

How Customers Helped One Organization Grow

After I got my MBA, I went to work in my family business. We had a solid business, but its growth was completely stalled. For three years in a row, it had done $3 million in

Understanding and Communicating Your Company's Identity and Purpose

volume. There seemed to be no way to break that cycle. But we did. In fact, we went from $3 million to $5 million to $10 million to $25 million in four years' time.

How did we accomplish those phenomenal results? We invited both our employees and customers into the process. Our company had five divisions. After consulting each one, we created a business plan and a vision statement for each division.

Our customers contributed insights about how we could work better with them and be much more customer-responsive than we had been before. And because our employees felt they were an important part of the process too, implementing the plan went smoothly.

Our plan predicted that we would grow from $3 million to $10 million in five years. In fact, we went from $3 million to $25 million in only four. With our customers as our partners, we were wildly successful at growing the business.

Create a Strategic Plan to Get to Where You Want to Go

A strategic plan is an important tool that can help your organization grow, achieve specific goals on a schedule, and reach its fullest potential. To define the goals and timelines that will be part of your plan, you will need to consult with your management team, appropriate managers and employees, vendors, customers and other stakeholders too. Also remember that a strategic plan should be grounded in your company's vision and mission statements, which reflect your values, higher goals and aspirations.

How far ahead should you be planning? Five years into the future is normally ideal. Your goals should be challenging and stretch you, while also being concrete and understandable. Goals that lie 10 or 20 years into the future become so esoteric that people cannot relate to them.

Now, are you really going to use one plan, accomplish everything that is in it, and then meet again in five years to write a new one? No, not really. I recommend creating a five-year plan, then meeting at least once a year to review it and ask some questions like these:

- Where are we now in executing this plan?
- Do we still want to pursue all the goals that it sets out, or have other priorities emerged that we should tackle first?
- What specific tactics do we need to work on in the next year so that we can accomplish our goals?

The status quo changes quickly in business today, and

you will need to revise your plan and keep your goals fresh. Yet there is great value in saying to people, "here are our goals for the next five years." This is especially true when you create specific initiatives, assignments, and tactics that people will address in the year to follow.

Here's an analogy that illustrates the importance of planning . . .

If you put 22 kids who have never played soccer before on a soccer field and you said to them, "Here's a soccer ball, have fun playing soccer," what kind of soccer game would it be? They wouldn't necessarily know there were two teams. They wouldn't know the rules or how to keep score. They might eventually start kicking the ball around, but the game of soccer wouldn't happen. But when you explain the game and that the goal is to put the ball in the net, then people achieve and accomplish something.

The same is true in business. When you're just doing the same things over again and no one has given you a goal or a plan, no one has told you how to score, you just keep doing the same things over and over again. You don't know what you should be doing and it's impossible to achieve any kind of success.

Concluding thoughts for this chapter...

As the Roman philosopher Seneca once wrote, "If a sailor does not know to which port he is sailing, no wind is favorable." Another way of saying that is that to get to the right place, you have to know what you and your organization want to achieve. That means defining your mission, vision and goals.

CHAPTER FIVE

Communication Skills for Ingaged Leadership

The single biggest problem in communication is the illusion that it has taken place.
- GEORGE BERNARD SHAW

Even the greatest techniques for ingaged leadership will not be effective until you communicate clearly and compellingly. We will take a look at how to do that in this chapter.

Ingaging Leadership

Most managers and top executives know that it takes a lot of work to communicate clearly. It requires:

- Effectively conveying the big picture
- Motivating people to participate and deliver their very best
- Communicating just the right amount of information – neither too much nor too little
- Sending the right messages to our teams
- Conveying instructions and ideas clearly
- Ingaging people in the process decision-making, not just telling them what to do
- Helping people understand not just what to do, but why they are doing it

Analyze Your Communications

How can you know if your company has good communications? Here are some signs to watch for in employees and managers:

- **An eagerness to communicate** - The staff enjoys and is enthusiastic about planning, meetings, simple conversations and the memos and communications that they receive from others in your organization.

- **Smooth communication** – Team members, managers and employees receive, understand, and take action on the information they receive. There is minimal need to repeat messages. People access your intranet, read your communications, and stay ingaged. As a result, top executives are able to ingage in higher-level pursuits like long-term planning, product development and cultivating new markets and customers.

- **Ambition and enterprise** - People are eager to get going on new initiatives, get work done, and help in the pursuit of organizational excellence.

- **Widespread understanding of bigger issues** - People don't only know what's happening on a day-to-day basis, they also understand the company's long-term goals, mission, vision and values. They take an active role in helping the company succeed.

- **Ability to execute** – People don't only start projects, they finish them. Few or no people do just enough to "get by."
- **Confidence and empowerment** - People believe in themselves, feel supported by management, and complacency has not set in.

Why Poor Communication Is Costly

According to "The High Cost of Poor Communication," a report from the 360 Solutions consulting organization, poor communication patterns are both costly and frustrating. The study found that in a company with 100 employees where inefficient communication patterns have taken hold, company leadership has to invest an average of 17 hours each week striving to clarify communication. That translates to an annual cost to the company of $528,443.

According to the study, some of the costliest forms of poor communication can be traced to closed-minded leaders who cut off feedback. The result is a culture that tolerates interruptions, negative body language, and even anger.

Keys to Building More Ingaged Personal Communication

Some of us start out as poor communicators and have to work hard to improve. Many of us start in the middle levels. A very few of us start out as highly effective communicators. But where we start is less important than our desire to improve our abilities.

How can you cultivate the habit of continuous improvement as a communicator? Here are some attitudes to think about, cultivate, and apply strategically:

- **When appropriate, start with no dependence** on achieving a specific outcome. Instead, intend for the highest good to come about. Remaining focused on specific outcomes can distract you from achieving a higher good.
- **Be curious** to hear more, know more, and to help others to learn.
- **Ask open-ended questions** that require more than a yes or no reply.
- **Probe the statements and answers** that you hear to get a full understanding. Don't assume you know what someone else means.

- **Try to understand** where other people are coming from, what is at stake for them, and ask questions to understand what their unspoken concerns may be.
- **Distinguish** fact from opinion. We will explore this issue in more depth in Chapter Five.
- **Be mentally present** to ensure that you understand what you're hearing.
- **Be conscious** when you are triggered (upset or angry) and learn to quickly set those feelings aside. Then return to your search for good ideas and solutions.
- **Take the time** to notice how others react to what you say.
- **Strive for solutions** that meet the needs of many people.
- **Be patient** in your communication and allow others to speak at a pace that is most natural to them.

Five Ways to Make People More Receptive to What You Are Saying

I once worked with an organization that distributed a recorded audio clip to its entire sales force. At the end of the recording, salespeople were asked to send an email to a specific administrative assistant. Each salesperson who listened to the entire clip until the end would learn that he or she had received a watch – and a pretty nice watch at that. Yet only two out of the 800 salespeople responded to that offer. They were the only ones who listened to the entire message. The rest of the salesmen and saleswomen didn't get that far. Unfortunately, this is a common problem.

But here are some strategies that will help ensure your employees are interested and involved in what you have to say:

- **Understand and communicate the "What's In It for Me" (WIIFM)** – People are more likely to read communications or act on them when they perceive a clear and immediate benefit from doing so.

- **Explain the "why"** – People will be more likely to act if they understand the reasons behind your communication.

- **Keep emails and other communications clear and simple** – Be organized, to the point.

- **Resist the temptation to repeat yourself unnecessarily** – People are far less likely to open or read your communications if they have learned that you will convey the same information over and over again.

- **Define roles and responsibilities** – State clearly who is on the team and explain their respective responsibilities.

Remember that performance reviews offer a good opportunity to evaluate each employee's skills as a communicator. If people need to improve or refine their skills, find workshops or professional educational courses that will help them.

The Junk Drawer Analogy

Do you have an intranet or communication portal for information, updates, company news, and other information? If so, pay special attention that information is current, brief, clear and worth reading.

Sadly, communication portals can easily resemble the "junk drawer" that many of us use to put stuff that we don't want to deal with. You know what that drawer is like. It contains everything, but finding what you're looking for can waste a lot of time. Sometimes you may have to empty the entire contents, only to discover that what you're looking for isn't even there.

Keep the Junk Drawer Analogy in mind when organizing communications within your organization. If you keep things uncluttered and simple, you will save a lot of time, improve efficiency and enjoy many other dividends.

Ingaging Leadership

Take Pains to Differentiate Fact from Opinion

This is a very critical issue for me. We are living in a time when many people express their opinions as if they were facts. Many do it unknowingly, others intentionally. We hear politicians do it. It has also become commonplace on talk radio and television news.

When people speak with any level of passion or conviction, they often speak as if what they are saying is a fact. In reality, much of what people try to pass off as facts are simply opinions. And when people state an opinion as a fact, their audience is prone to believe it to be a fact and react to it in a certain way. Most often, the conversation either ends or never gets to the point of addressing real issues.

You might hear someone in your organization say, for example, "You cannot bring that product to market by early next year because of A, B, and C." That person is stating opinions as though they were facts and if you disagree, you look like you are calling him or her a liar.

If you cultivate the habit of delineating between fact and opinion during conversations, you become more empowered to move toward real solutions. If you fail to do so, miscommunications usually result. Imagine, for example, that you're asking for advice about a particular issue, but that you express your opinion of that situation as though it were undisputable truth. In such a case, the advice that you receive will probably not have great merit, because the other person will not base his or her advice on a wider and more comprehensive understanding of what the situation really is.

From the other side of the equation, it is wise to cast a similarly critical eye on the information you receive, by consistently challenging the assumption that what is being said or presented to you is actually fact. To make the most informed decisions, you need to investigate and become as certain as you can that you are considering not opinions, but the reality of what is taking place.

Now, it's not realistic to think you can do this with absolutely everything that comes across your desk or in every conversation. Time limitations and pressures often will keep you from probing on a deep level into what you are hearing. And you do not need to do so all the time – not when you are dealing with low-priority issues or activities, for example. But you certainly should do it when you are dealing with serious or deep issues. That's where you'll want to dig deeper – to look at every angle to get to the real facts.

When you get there, you'll realize a significant improvement in business. Fact or opinion? You decide.

Communications skills that help differentiate opinions from facts . . .

- When you are offering an opinion, precede it with the phrase, "In my opinion." This differentiates opinions from facts. Perhaps more importantly, it raises the quality of the conversation by inviting people to contribute to your opinion, refute it, or offer productive alternatives of their own.

- **Ask other people, "Is what you are saying a fact or an opinion?"** This strategy, like the one just above, encourages others to be more alert to situations in which they are tempted to offer their opinions as facts.

- **Point out when other people** are presenting opinions as facts. This can be difficult to do because in a way, you are pointing out that those other people might be lying. Plus, it can be unpleasant to challenge other people's opinions. If someone says, for example, "Your price increases are killing sales," you should consider exposing that statement by stating that it is an opinion, not a fact. You can then explore that opinion to see if it has validity or is simply an attempt to box you into a corner or limit a productive search for information and solutions. In some cases, you will discover the other person is simply trying to advance his or her own agenda or goals. One good choice of words is to say, "I believe . . ." ("I believe that other factors could be at work too . . . let's explore some more.") In a non-confrontational way, those words help you address the reality that another person is expressing an opinion as though it were a fact.

- **Get into the habit** of looking for facts. If someone says, "Your price increases are killing sales," you can work with that person to arrive at statistics, data, feedback, and facts that either support or refute the opinion. This elevates the quality of your conversation to a level of higher ingagement.

> **ACTION STEPS**
>
> Over the next two days, pay attention to times when people state opinions as facts. Watch some commentary shows on television and notice when it's taking place. Pay attention to your own communication too, and try to make sure that others know when you are stating an opinion. What do these steps tell you about how effectively you and other people in your organization make this important distinction?

Fight the Tendency to Make Assumptions when Communicating

As executives, we are often pressured to find immediate solutions to problems that we are facing. We therefore have to fight the natural temptation to make quick assumptions.

For example, we tend to have preconceived notions about the effectiveness of what we are doing, often based on what has been effective in the past. If staffers aren't complaining about our management style or systems, we assume that people like them. By the same token, we tend to make assumptions about what other people are doing. If sales are going pretty well, we assume the people we have hired are doing a good job of selling.

Yet we can challenge our assumptions and encourage others to follow suit. I am not talking about micromanaging. I am stressing the importance of remaining aware and hands-on as an executive or manager, in appropriate and involved ways. How? Keep talking, reviewing, and communicating with the people in your organization. Consistent, regular and ingaged communication is key, and here is one effective way to achieve it . . .

Invest Energy to Become a Good Listener

Are you a good listener? A "real" good listener? Or do distracting thoughts make your mind wander during meetings? Do you become defensive and tend to find fault with others? Are you a selective listener, looking to prove that others are wrong and you are right?

Communication Skills for Ingaged Leadership

A good way to overcome those inhibitors is to be purposeful in your conversation by building these skills:

- **Remain mentally present during conversations.** Focus on what the other person is saying.

- **Don't interrupt or rush to reply.** Be sure the other person is finished speaking before you respond. It is helpful to take a breath while considering your next comment instead of speaking completely off the cuff. This is especially important when discussing sensitive or emotional topics.

- **Acknowledge the positive.** Then build on it by digging deeper.

- **Analyze communications that have taken place.** Consider what went well, what could have gone better, and how to improve next time.

When you do these things, you will have better conversations, deeper relationships and better outcomes. You will spend more time looking for the little nuggets of high value during your conversations and use them to stay focused on positive results.

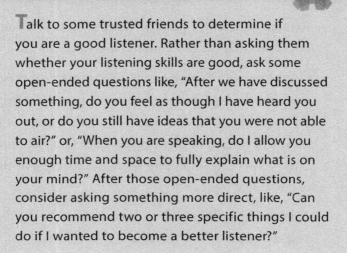

ACTION STEP

Talk to some trusted friends to determine if you are a good listener. Rather than asking them whether your listening skills are good, ask some open-ended questions like, "After we have discussed something, do you feel as though I have heard you out, or do you still have ideas that you were not able to air?" or, "When you are speaking, do I allow you enough time and space to fully explain what is on your mind?" After those open-ended questions, consider asking something more direct, like, "Can you recommend two or three specific things I could do if I wanted to become a better listener?"

Concluding thoughts for this chapter . . .

As you have read this chapter, have you discovered any areas where you need to improve as a communicator? Every small improvement that you make in the effectiveness of your communication will quickly repay you with remarkable and rewarding improvements.

CHAPTER SIX

Mastering The Three Types of Communication

We communicate all the time at work. We speak face-to-face, talk on the phone, send emails, attend meetings, chat in kitchenettes and cafeterias, and more. Yet the best leaders and managers don't let their communication just "happen." They adapt their style of communication to achieve desired outcomes.

In this chapter, we will explore a new way to think about the process of communication – a way of thinking that that can lead to more ingaged and effective leadership.

I will present a way to understand and explore three distinct types of communication. Why am I devoting a chapter to three levels of communication that I have identified? Let me explain. When you learn to recognize the three types of communication:

- **You will be in a better position to understand the people you lead.** If people are being evasive and covering up information, for example, you will be better able to discern that is taking place. Even more importantly, you will be in a better position to understand their motivations, to lift their communication to a higher level, and to lead them more insightfully and ingagingly.
- **You will become a more genuine, positive and ingaged leader.** I believe that when leaders distort the

truth (which is a kinder way of saying that they are lying), they damage their own ability to lead in many ways that are not immediately apparent. If you develop the habit of telling small lies, like telling people that their reports are due tomorrow when next week is time enough, you might not get caught telling a lie. But over time, your authenticity as a leader will erode, because people's intuition will subtly alert them that you are not as authentic a leader as you seem to be. Getting in the habit of distorting the truth, omitting information, and engaging in other small forms of lying can also weaken your resolve to lead on the highest, most ethical level.

When you understand them, they can help you communicate much more effectively and build more ingaged leadership. In a sense, this chapter's content is an extension of the communication skills that we explored in the previous chapter. Yet I believe that these additional concepts are so important they deserve a chapter of their own.

Type 1 – Evasive Communication

Most of the communication that takes place in this category has to do with lying. There are three sub-categories of communication that take place within Evasive Communication:

Mastering The Three Types of Communication

- **Straight-out lying** – When people communicate in this way, their actions show an attitude of, "I lie habitually, without provocation."

- **Defensive lying** – "When I am being questioned or feel threatened, I lie to cover myself. I often do it without much thought, it just happens."

- **Withholding information (not telling the whole truth)** – "I am avoiding certain topics, or not responding or contributing pertinent information when someone else is talking with me." This most often occurs when someone is trying to influence a conversation so that it results in a decision that he or she prefers.

Despite the fact that this is the least effective type communication, there are still times when positive leaders adapt it to save time. Many of those times are rooted in customs – the ways we habitually interact in our society.

Let's say, for example, that a colleague comes into my office one day and asks, "How are you?" It happens that I am not feeling too well that day. But there is no good reason to say, "Since you asked, I have a headache, I think I might be getting a cold, and I am grumpy." No, in the interest of efficiency, I will probably just answer, "Doing ok, felt better," and then get into the substance of our meeting. We all take part in that kind of communication every day, in which it is pointless and time wasting to respond with complete honesty.

At the same time, it is critically important to think carefully and critically before choosing to omit or shape information to achieve certain results. For example, I have known salespeople who called into their companies and lied about the orders they place. One told his company that a client "Needed to have his order delivered by the end of the month" when in fact, the customer had never made that demand. This salesperson wanted the order to be delivered so he could make his monthly sales quota and earn a commission on the sale sooner.

You might think there was no harm in what that salesperson did – he lied to reach certain goals. Yet what would have happened if his lie were uncovered – if, for example, the customer called the salesperson's supervisor and said that he had never requested a delivery by month's end. If that happened, the salesperson's credibility and reputation would have been destroyed, both with his client and with his company. It is always wisest to look at how you are communicating and ask, "Can this lie cause damage?"

Consider the damage that results when people within an organization get in the habit of lying defensively to protect themselves. Unfortunately, this is not uncommon. Someone fails to notice an email, therefore fails to execute an important project, and then tells everyone, "I never got that email." Or someone forgets to make an important phone call and later lies, "I left a message, but nobody returned my call."

Let's face it. At one time or another, it's tempting to stretch the truth or avoid it altogether to avoid blame. This

Mastering The Three Types of Communication

behavior can do more harm than you might expect. Severe operational problems take root in companies where lying has become commonplace. The real and deeper problem is that in such organizations, management becomes cut off from what's really going on and cannot respond to problems that should be addressed.

Although in some cases "white lies" of withholding information may be benign, that's not always the case. This is another reason why it is so important to uncover, evaluate and influence communication in your organization.

ACTION STEPS

When have you been evasive and why? What was the result? Remember, there are times when withholding information can be practical. It is not necessary to share every detail of information in every situation, after all. Be aware, however, that people who are habitually evasive—who constantly try to "cover their backs"—can do a lot of harm to your organization.

Quick assessment exercise

- Can you think of a time when you practiced evasive communication? Did you do so intentionally, or by force of habit? What were the results?

- Can you think of a time when someone else practiced in evasive communication? What happened, and were the outcomes good or bad?

Type 2 – Conclusive Communication

If I am at participating in communication of this type, I am actually speaking honestly. However, I am not communicating authentically, because I am trying to direct the conversation and achieve a specific result. I am shaping the way I communicate because I have unspoken goals and motives that I am trying to advance.

There are three sub-categories of communication within Conclusive Communication:

- **Impulsive self-interest.** – When people communicate in this way, their actions show an attitude of, "I say what is on my mind without much thought or concern to the purpose of the conversation or interests of the person I am talking to. Many times this happens when a conversation erupts before I have had a chance to think first about what I will say. I am supposed to be listening to the person I am talking to, but instead I am only concerned with what I am thinking."
- **Defending a position or goal.** – "I am expressing my true thoughts and I understand the purpose of the conversation and the other person's desires and goals. However, I am

Mastering The Three Types of Communication

not willing to truly consider anyone else's point of view. I am either fighting for my point of view or defending it."

- **Seeking to blame and find fault.** – "I am asking good questions and acting like I truly care about the other person's point of view. But my real goal is to use what the person is saying to either prove I have listened or to find ammunition to defeat his or her point of view. I am not really open to changing my mind; I just try to manipulate the person I am talking to."

As I wrote at the start of this chapter, applying those communications styles at the wrong times can diminish your authenticity and credibility as a leader. There are other times, however, when leaders must make the decision not to take part in completely open and receptive communication.

- **One example:** Your company operations manual states that your company opens its door for business every day at 8:00 A.M. One day an employee arrives an hour late and says, "I feel tired, I think that starting tomorrow, we should begin opening our doors at 9:00." If that happens, my response as a manger will not be to say, "Please tell me why you think it would be better to start opening an hour later?" and then engage in a lengthy discussion about it, because in order for my company to continue doing business, we need to follow our operating procedures. (If your employees have a big meeting every year to review our procedures and norms, that is the place to discuss changing our hours of operation, not on a situational basis.)

- **Another example:** As a manager, you need one of the people you supervise to do something in the next 20 minutes, like calling up a vendor to ask when an important shipment will arrive. You are not going to ask the employee, "Can you tell me in depth how you really feel about calling the vendor?" Similarly, if your supervisor asks you to do something quickly, the best idea is probably just to do it. If you want to discuss the nature of the task or your job in more depth, you should pick another time.

- **Another example:** Complete openness and honesty are sometimes not ideal when you are negotiating an agreement with someone whose goals are in opposition to yours. Let's say, for instance, that you and your attorneys are trying to negotiate a financial settlement with a company that has infringed on a patent that you hold. You have your position, so does the other side, and it is not a time to ask questions like, "Tell me how you feel about paying us what we are owed." The people on the other side will doubtless be pressing for their own agenda and needs too, and your strong position can only benefit you.

Mastering The Three Types of Communication

Quick assessment exercise:

Can you think of a time when you took part in conclusive communication?

- If you have communicated in this way, was it intentional? If so, why?
- How useful were the outcomes?
- Who in your organization uses this type of communication, either habitually or from time to time? What effect are they having on your company culture, efficiency and success?

Type 3 – Openness and Honesty

If I have reached this type of communication, I am speaking openly, without being tied to a result. I am willing to allow others' ideas and thoughts to play an equal part alongside mine in the conversation. Again, there are three categories of communication within this type of communication:

- Not fully involved in the process of changing my mind. – When people communicate in this way, their actions show an attitude of, "I am fully honest in conversation, clearly creating a distinction between the facts and my opinions. I listen to what the other person has to say, but I stop short of pulling their whole thoughts from them. I am only somewhat open to changing my mind, not actively committed to the process of exchanging ideas and contributions."

- **Willingness to change my mind.** – "I present facts first and then opinions. I clearly delineate the differences between the two. I communicate with high clarity. I am concerned for the other person's point of view. I ask open-ended questions to fully understand them. And I am fully open to a change in my opinion."

- **Clarity and openness.** – "I go into conversations with no defined outcomes in mind, not even a preferred direction that I might be willing to change. I have a totally open mind. I concern myself not only with the statements that the other person is making. I also try to really understand the other person's underlying intent. I consider what is at stake for the person I am talking to and what his or her concerns and goals are. When I ask questions, I listen to the answers with true curiosity. I follow up on the answers I hear by asking deeper and more probing questions that help me fully understand the other person's point of view. I clearly delineate the difference between fact and my own opinion. I may get triggered (experience strong, unproductive feelings) when the other person states a position that differs from mine, but I am able to set my trigger aside; I know that their viewpoints are as legitimate as mine are, so I strive to find the fit between what they see and what I see. My goal is for the mutually best outcome."

This is a level of informed and active communication that is worth striving for in many situations. If I am interacting with a colleague whose input and ideas can lead to improved operations within my organization, I want to be at this level in my communication – not to get stuck at lower levels because of my own habits or those of the person I am working with.

When you are taking part in true leadership activities, you should be able to practice communication at this very high level. Only through highly evolved communication abilities can you lead any organization to achieve its fullest potential. But having mastered those skills, wise leaders know how to weigh and apply them in the service of efficiency and results.

Quick assessment exercise:

- Are you able to take part in open and honest communication? If not, can you pinpoint any roadblocks that are holding you back?
- If you have engaged in open and honest communication, were the outcomes good or bad?

- Are there people in your organization who take part in open and honest communication at this level, either habitually or from time to time? If so, what effect are they having on your company culture, efficiency and success?
- If you were able to strategically achieve this level of communication within your organization, what do you believe the results would be?

> **ACTION STEP**
>
> Think of a conversation you had when you were conclusive—and when you could have benefitted from being more open and honest. If you could now repeat that talk at a higher level, how might the results have differed?

A Final Word on Communicating Effectively in the Three Types...

I have observed that when it comes to communicating at these different levels, you get what you give, and you give what you get.

That is a way of saying that if you begin a conversation with someone using one of the types of communication that

I describe in this chapter, he or she will tend to communicate with you at that same level. If I start a conversation at a particular level of conclusive communication, for example, that other person will tend to adopt that level, too. And if I start lying to protect myself, that other person will probably do the same. But on the positive side, if I make a statement like, "I really want to hear your best ideas and suggestions . . . do you have a few minutes to spend with me?" people will rise to that style of communication.

Concluding thoughts for this chapter . . .

Spend some time thinking about the concepts that we have covered in this chapter – the different types of communication that we have explored.

After I have explained them to executives and managers, most of them have told me shortly afterwards that their effectiveness has immediately improved. They have saved time, motivated people more effectively, lowered the level of frustration that comes with inefficient communicating, and enjoyed other benefits. If you would like to experience a dramatic improvement in your leadership, the skills in this chapter are a good place to start.

CHAPTER SEVEN

Building a Strong and Ingaged Team

Effective leaders build their success by partnering with people. They take steps to recruit the right people and cultivate them after they are on board. In this chapter, we will explore effective ways to build a great team.

Ingagement is not something that happens only at the top of your organization, or with individual managers at different levels. For ingagement to reach its fullest potential it should become part of your organization's DNA.

Let's take a moment to revisit "Employee Engagement: What's Your Engagement Ratio," a study conducted by the Gallup Organization that I mentioned in Chapter Two. To recap, that research found that an increase of 70% in employee engagement yields a 240% increase in customer engagement. Companies with high levels of engagement achieve earnings per share growth at a rate that is 3.9 times greater than do companies with poor employee engagement.

To quote from that study:

> *"The world's top-performing organizations understand that employee engagement is a force that drives business outcomes. Research shows that engaged employees are more productive employees. They are more profitable, more customer-focused,*

safer, and more likely to withstand temptations to leave the organization. In the best organizations, employee engagement transcends a human resources initiative — it is the way they do business."

To summarize, ingaged employees are far more effective than non-ingaged employees. They think and act differently. They are more collaborative, more concerned about the success of your company. They also create a very positive work environment.

Simply wanting ingaged employees is not the key. The key is to cultivate ingagement in the people who work in your organization, and also to hire the right people. That's what this chapter is all about.

How Can You Cultivate a High Level of Ingagement?

To run a successful organization, you need to bring together a mix of people with a variety of strengths. Another way of stating it is that you need variety, as embodied in a group of people who possess different strengths.

One reason to cultivate a good mix is that we all have weaknesses. Everyone in any organization has shortcomings in terms of needed skills, and it is important to recruit people who can help compensate for them.

For example, I am a person who doesn't like to get "in the weeds," by which I mean I don't always relish handling the day-to-day, operational side of my business, although I can handle it capably when I absolutely have to. But I bring a negative attitude to such tasks, and I tend to make mistakes. It is hardly a win-win situation. That is why I have balanced my staff by recruiting people who are incredibly detail-oriented. I can share a big idea – most often, one that they have helped me develop in an ingaged way. They then can help turn that idea into a tactical plan and actually make it work.

So the goal is to create a balanced staff that allows everyone to spend the majority of their time doing what they are really good at, and what they enjoy.

The Problem with Hiring People Who Are Just Like You

Many company owners, managers and executives make the mistake of hiring people who are just like they are, or putting together teams of similarly minded people. Software engineers tend to like to work with other software engineers, for example, and people who launched businesses by selling assertively tend to hire assertive sales professionals. As a result, their organizations fail to have the balance that they need for peak performance.

Instead, take a look at what's happening within your organization. As you look at your team, do you see people who are doing only what they are required to do, rather than what they love to do and at which they excel? If that is the case, your company as well as your team could be better served if you recruited a mix of people who together provided all the skills necessary.

Imagine that your business is like a symphony orchestra. Now imagine your orchestra is made up only of musicians who can play strings and tympani. What kind of music will it make? Granted, it might sound okay, but it will not make beautiful music. A full symphony orchestra usually has a group of musicians who play more than 13 different instruments, not just one or two. And chances are that your organization needs people who can perform a dozen or more specific roles.

ACTION STEP

Consider the variety of the people in your company. Are there gaps in ability, attitude or experience that are preventing your organization from achieving its greatest potential? If you were starting up today, what kind of staff would allow the business to grow and prosper?

Building a Strong and Ingaged Team

When considering your business teams, think of yourself as a conductor who, with the right mix of ingaged people and a beautiful score, can achieve brilliant success.

Hire and Support People Who Have the Right Attitude

Attitude is the most important trait among your people. Attitude is a game-changer. If you populate your organization with people who are positive, they will lift others and lead them to excel. On the other side of the equation, negative people can drain the energy out of everyone around them. Negative people in an organization can kill your chances of success.

I am not recommending that you want a staff made up of people who are irrationally positive all the time – artificially upbeat cheerleaders who have no grounding in practical business. I am saying that you want resilient people who adopt a strongly positive yet realistic point of view when facing business challenges and setbacks. Those will be the same people who will look for ways to make things even better in times when everything seems to be going well.

Negativism kills. You can talk to some very skilled people who will say, "I know that everything seems to be going well right now, but I am waiting for the other shoe to drop . . .

here are a few negative things that are bound to happen, and things will then get worse."

Although it is good to look ahead and anticipate future problems, you want people who are going to be positive, who are going to realistically inspire others. And when people are inspired, they will perform better and your enterprise will prosper.

Evaluate and Compare Employee Attitudes

Ron Willingham, the author of Integrity Selling for the 21st Century and other excellent books, has devised a very simple way to evaluate the effect of attitude on team members:

- **First,** evaluate the person's expertise – how much he or she knows – on a scale of 1 to 10.

- **Second,** evaluate his or her experience – how long has he or she been doing this kind or work – again on a scale of 1 to 10.

- **Third,** assess his or her attitude on a scale of 1 to 10.

- **Fourth,** add together the numbers from the first two steps, and multiply the result by the number from the third step.

Sample evaluations:

- **Employee A** rates an 8 in expertise, an 8 in experience, and a 2 in attitude. Her overall score is then 16. [(8+8) x 2 = 16]
- **Employee B** rates a 2 in expertise, a 4 in experience, and an 8 in attitude. His overall score is then 48. [(2+4) x 8 = 48]

Willingham's approach reveals that you can hire someone who has skills relevant to your needs and 30 years of experience, but who will still not create value for you if he or she has a negative attitude.

If you hire someone who has a can-do attitude and very little experience, he or she can have the potential to be much more productive than a negative employee with far greater experience and skill.

Make a Commitment to Invest in People

Unless you have highly motivated people who understand your company's vision and are committed to it, it will be difficult for your organization to achieve its fullest potential.

If you don't already think of your people as resources to be cultivated, I urge you to start doing so by applying some or all of the practices that follow.

Create a Plan for Each Employee

The people who work for and with you are always changing, always in a state of flux. Some are improving, others are following a downward path. Some are becoming more committed to your organization, while others are growing dissatisfied. Some are developing new skills and discovering better ways of supporting your company, while others are burning out and looking for jobs elsewhere. Good companies understand that change is part of working and become committed to cultivating employees so they consistently take the higher road and improve.

Employees' performance reviews offer a good setting to cooperatively create plans with them. What specific goals would employees like to reach in the coming year and beyond? What skills and experiences would you like them to add? If you put those expectations onto a timeline, you will have taken a good step toward helping your employees grow, become more fulfilled in their work and become more valuable to your organization too.

> **ACTION STEP**
>
> Identify several employees in your organization who would benefit if you created development plans for them. Next, write down some of the steps that you would include in that plan, such as training, spending time in other company locations, and more. After that, try to identify more employees who could benefit if you created a plan for each of them. Finally, make some decisions about whether, when and how you might create those plans.

Invest Wisely in Training

Training creates a company where people have superior skills, yet training can pay even larger benefits. One of the biggest is that if you invest in training, your employees will realize that they have a future with your company. That creates an environment where your best people are much more dedicated, loyal and productive.

A joke that conveys a deeper meaning . . .

A manager asks, "What if I invest a lot of money in training my people and then they leave me?"

Another manager retorts, "What if you don't train them and they stay?"

The reality is, it's critical to have a well-trained staff if you want better performance. Yet many companies unfortunately scrimp on training.

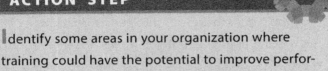

ACTION STEP

Identify some areas in your organization where training could have the potential to improve performance dramatically. Make a plan to provide it.

Perform Regular Reviews

Reviews help ensure that the people in your organization understand your expectations and your opinions about how they are doing. Here are some other reasons why reviews are such effective tools:

- Reviews help keep people and their work aligned with current company priorities and plans, so they are not "working blind."
- Reviews can provide important information you need to know about any current personal problems or issues that could be affecting employees' work.

Building a Strong and Ingaged Team

- Reviews offer a good setting where you and employees can make motivational plans for what they should achieve in the coming six months or year.

- Reviews offer an opportunity to "take employees' temperatures" about how positive they feel, how ingaged they are, and other issues.

How are you doing in this regard? If you are not conducting regular reviews, you could be causing more problems with your team members than you realize. Why? One reason is that, in my opinion, people tend to believe the worst, not the best, if they are kept in the dark about your evaluation of them.

Two effective ways to conduct reviews

- **Self-evaluation prior to review** - The manager and the employee each completes a review form, then meet some days later to compare and discuss their comments. In my experience, when employees evaluate themselves in preparation for a review, they do not hesitate to be critical of themselves. Though they tend to bring up areas that I wanted to raise anyway, they often are harder on themselves than I would be.

- **360° reviews** - Each employee is reviewed by not only him or herself and a supervisor, but by a group of people with whom he or she interacts on the job. My preferred way of conducting these reviews is to have people submit their evaluations of the team member who will be reviewed, then to sort the comments into categories on one master form. That prevents the employee under evaluation from trying to guess the identity of his or her evaluators. And 360° reviews can be very effective. If an employee sees that a number of people are focusing on an area that needs improvement, those comments will be more credible than those that came from one supervisor. On the opposite side of the equation, when an employee sees that people like what he or she is doing, those positive comments are more believable and encouraging.

Some insights from a sample 360° review . . .

A 360 review can communicate a wealth of information. Here are some comments I received about my own strengths and areas for potential improvement during one of my reviews:

- "As a leader, Evan is first rate. He is respectful of people and solicits opinion. He also does a good job of keeping management in the loop on high level strategic thinking and direction."

- "Evan is a strong leader with a vision. He manages different people differently according to their personality and needs. He is very responsive to staff and to members. He is very good about communicating and sharing what's going on with staff and members. He is a very hands-on manager. He is also a very inclusive manager and one who wants to get both staff and membership more involved (e.g. many councils, monthly staff meetings)."

- "Evan is learning how to ask more questions to let others get to the right answers instead of trying to manipulate issues toward what he feels is the right path."

- "Spend more time communicating up front. This was done very well with the five-year plan, but it could be extended further. Also, I believe Evan is one of the most compassionate leaders that I have met, but this does not always come across with members and some staff members. It would be helpful if he would take the time to explain things with a little more clarity."

While that feedback isn't always pretty, it is always useful. It has been invaluable to my own interpersonal and management development. These reviews can energize your staff members too, and further the process of consistent improvement.

Two strategies to help you and your employees benefit much more from reviews...

Let me share two strategies that I have found to improve can dramatically improve the review process:

- **Bring the company's vision into the review discussion.** In reviews, I ask, "In your own words, what is the vision of the company?" I next ask, "How do you help the company achieve that vision?" Those two questions help assure that people understand the company vision, understand that it is important, and understand how they contribute.

- **Give new employees a copy of the review form as soon as you hire them.** This lets them know right away what they will be reviewed on. It also prevents the situation that often crops up in reviews when employees who have just gotten the form say, "I had no idea you were going to be reviewing me on these things!"

Add a plan to take reviews one step further...

Reviews are more than scorecards. They provide an opportunity to build a plan with each employee. What are the key areas the employee should focus on in the next year, for example? What is he or she doing well that can be built upon? What areas of improvement can they work on in the next 12 months? Once you've agreed together on goals, set check-in points and incorporate them in a training and development plan. Regardless of the type of review you choose, it can produce motivating action plans for learning and growth.

> **ACTION STEP**
>
> Assess the way your organization conducts reviews. Consider regularity, approach, methodology, and look for areas ripe for improvements.

Remember that Benefits Matter

Offering excellent benefits to the people in your company is expensive – no question – but it is critical to cultivating and retaining a strong employee base. And as we noted at the start of this chapter, your staff is your greatest asset.

Benefits keep people within your organization. If you are not providing comprehensive healthcare coverage and another company offers a better package, people in your company will look for work at that other company. The same is true in relation to funding a 401(k).

Investing in benefits ultimately means that you will keep good people and reduce your turnover. And remember, turnover is expensive. To find a replacement for an employee who leaves is expensive and time-wasting. You have to spend money and time to recruit each new employee – usually while the job of the employee who left is being handled by other staffers, or being left undone. After you bring your new employee on board, it costs money for the training that gets him or her up to speed. And in some cases, the first person you hire doesn't work out. He or she fails to serve customers well while getting up to speed, for one example, which costs you money and business. And if that new hire doesn't work out, you have to repeat the entire process a second or even a third time.

Those steps are hugely expensive. Yet in many cases, you can prevent them by simply having an excellent benefits plan.

I have been a small businessperson and I have worked for large companies, too. I am fully aware of how time-consuming and expensive it is for small businesses to offer good benefits. But the reality is that doing so is worth it. The money you invest is money well spent.

ACTION STEP

Review your benefits plan by comparing it to those that are being offered by other companies where your employees could be looking for jobs. If your benefits aren't in the ballpark, you could be encouraging your people to leave you.

Look for Value Fit

Even the most skilled and hardworking employees might not be the best people for your organization if their values do not fit with those of your company. If your company's values include a commitment to listening to customers and exceeding their needs, for example, a manager who doesn't like to listen to customers might not be the best person to have on your staff, even if he or she seems to be meeting the requirements of the job.

When an employee is a solid performer and does not fit the corporate values, you face a difficult challenge. Unfortunately, such employees are unlikely to change just because you tell them to "be more collaborative" or, "spend more time being an active listener." You can however, provide educational, training or other opportunities for them to learn to be more collaborative or improve their communication skills.

Some value problems might be insurmountable. Dishonesty and a lack of integrity, for example, are causes for termination.

It might be a controversial idea but in my opinion, when people reach a certain age, maybe age 30, it can be more difficult for them to change the way they think. They have grown up learning a certain set of values, and changing those values is hard for them and for you as an executive.

Strategies for Recruiting and Hiring Ingaged Staff Members

This book is not meant to be a handbook on hiring. There are many excellent books out there that are. However, I would like to offer some suggestions on hiring the right people, from my perspective, that can help you cultivate a more ingaged organization.

To evaluate listening...

Chances are that you will not gain too much insight into a job candidate's listening skills by asking, "Are you a good listener?" But you can learn a lot by paying attention to how well people listen during interviews. When you ask open-ended questions, do they listen well enough to respond directly to the questions you ask, as well as to any subtext?

To evaluate openness...

As you know, ingagement is the central theme of this book. Yet in interviews, it can be difficult to evaluate a job candidate's desire to communicate in the open and committed way that supports ingagement.

You could say something like, "In our company, we value openness. Do you value openness?" Yet because the person you are interviewing would like to be hired, chances are the he or she will reply, "Oh yes, very much, I value it." (Can-

Building a Strong and Ingaged Team

didates are unlikely to say, "I know it is a core value of your company, but I don't value it.")

The following questions can help you assess how open the person has been in the past, and on how much value he or she places on openness:

- "Tell me about a time when a colleague or manager couldn't deal with opinions that differed from his or hers? What did you do?"
- "In what areas in our company do you think openness would be helpful? Where would it be ineffective?"
- "What are some examples from your career that would demonstrate that you value openness?"
- "Can you tell me about a work situation when someone's openness and honesty have been beneficial?"

Those are probing and effective questions. I have noticed that it is difficult for candidates to lie on the spot or misrepresent themselves while answering them.

Question to evaluate other key areas . . .

- **To evaluate orientation toward results** - "Tell me about a time when something you got done demonstrated your focus on results."
- **To evaluate honesty** - "Share an example of a time when someone acted dishonestly. What did you do,

what were the results, and can you tell me what your take-away lesson was?"

- **To evaluate the desire to collaborate** - "Have you collaborated with other people to solve a problem? What did you learn that you believe could apply to working here?"

When you ask people to reflect on past experiences with questions like those, you elicit deeper information about what they believe and practice. You also have an improved ability to understand how well they will fit in your organization.

Concluding thoughts for this chapter...

Many employees will respond to the strategies that I explain in this book and become fully ingaged in your organization. But while I hesitate to end this chapter on a negative note, I would like to observe that there are times when letting the wrong people go sooner rather than later is the wisest decision you can make.

Although his slide caused people to laugh, it became somewhat clear in the discussion that followed that most of the people in the room believed in what it said – and believed that they could benefit from letting certain people go.

Building a Strong and Ingaged Team

> **ACTION STEP**
>
> I recently attended an excellent presentation by Jeremy McKinley, a very smart man who is a member of the top marketing team at Trek Bicycle. He was discussing his strategies for marketing and brand success. One of his slides said simply, "Fire Someone—You Know Who It Is."

If someone does not share company values (or does not care to do so), if he or she has shown dishonesty, if he or she is autocratic and uninterested in ingaging with the other members of your team, letting that person go can be a very wise decision indeed.

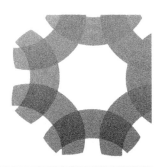

Conclusion

You have explored many concepts in this book. It is my hope that you are excited about what you have read. You have discovered what ingaged leadership is, why it is effective, and how to use it. You have also discovered action steps along the way to help you put ingaged leadership into daily practice.

But where should you begin? I would suggest that you start with areas where you have identified areas of opportunity as you have read these pages – concepts that made you think, "This is an area that could produce some excellent results for me if I address it now."

I would suggest that it would be best to start with two or three ideas, write them down, commit to doing them, make a plan for each, and execute them well.

Bringing other people into that process is very important. Say, "I just read this book and I feel that we should now do these things."

When you bring other people into the process, you greatly increase the likelihood the changes you want to make will actually happen. That is almost always the case.

An example from my non-business, personal life illustrates the point. I am a man of variable weight and every now and then, I need to go on a diet. When I tell people I am going to do that, I do really well. But when I go on what I call "secret diets" and tell myself, "I am just going to do it on my own," then the meal comes and I end up saying, "I'll start tomorrow." Then tomorrow comes and I say, "I'll start the following day." But sharing my plans brings success.

If you pick a few ideas from this book and commit to implementing them and share that commitment with your people, that is how change will happen.

And then after you have accomplished the first two or three things that you committed to, pick up the book again and pick two or three more key things, and then implement them.

Epilogue to the Second Print Edition

I have been receiving many positive comments and suggestions from many readers since this book was first released less than a year ago. I want to acknowledge those readers here and let them know that they have been heard. In fact, that input has resulted in a number of improvement in the preceding sections of this book.

But here, in a separate Epilogue, I would like to shed special light on several of the suggestions that readers have shared with me.

A Free Study Guide Is Now Available

Some readers have told me that they have begun to use *Ingaging Leadership* as a tool to build teams at work. Others have told me that they are discussing the book in book groups, professional organizations and other setting. In response, we have just published a special Book Discussion Guide that serves as a companion o the main volume. You can download a copy of it for free on the Ingage Consulting website.

> **ACTION STEP**
>
> Download the free Study Guide at Ingage.com (http://www.ingage.net/ingagingleadership/) and start discussing Ingaging Leadership within your company. Don't just focus on senior leadership, share this book with an inspiring leader in your company and see what happens. After you have explored this book, go on to study *The Energy Bus* by Jon Gordon and *The Fred Factor* by Mark Sanborn.

Widening the Lens on Leadership

Even though I envisioned this book as a book about leadership with a focus on business, people have told me that they are applying its lessons in their communities, charitable work and elsewhere. I value that perspective, because life affords us many opportunities to lead beyond the sphere of professional life.

I was particularly happy that several people suggested that the book's principles of Ingaged Leadership could be applied in very positive ways to family life.

Epilogue to the Second Print Edition

How can you use the Ingagement philosophy in your family? I would like to explain one very positive approach to Ingagement that I have used in my own family. I call it "Three Things," and I would like to recommend it to you. Here is how it works...

The Power of Three Things

A few years ago, I started to ask everyone at my family's dinner table to describe three positive things that had happened to them during the course of the day. I don't think they understood exactly why I was doing that – I probably didn't grasp the full importance of it either at the time.

At first, my children were a little skeptical, maybe even a little resistant. Their attitude conveyed an unspoken thought, "Oh, Dad... why should I have to do this?"

But then they seemed to warm to the idea. Even more importantly, they realized that they needed to be on the lookout for good things during the course of the day, because they knew we would be discussing them at dinner. That expectation created a big change in the way we were all experiencing our days. We were looking for good things, so instead of seeing the world through negative eyeglasses, we began to see it through positive ones.

After all, so many of us have developed the habit of seeing our day in terms of the negatives, and that is what we talk about. We had a bad day at work, the checkout lines were long at the grocery, the train home was delayed, the other drivers were crazy. We miss the positives. But with a simple shift, we can learn to turn around that way of thinking and seeing the world.

I would encourage you to experiment with Three Things, and to let me know the effect it has on you and those around you.

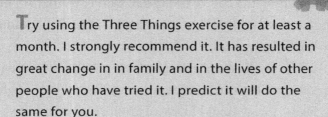

ACTION STEP

Try using the Three Things exercise for at least a month. I strongly recommend it. It has resulted in great change in in family and in the lives of other people who have tried it. I predict it will do the same for you.

Using the Power of the Positive to Become a Better Leader

You can certainly apply the Three Things at work. But for business communications, let me suggest expanding those three things to five. Let me explain how it works.

I recommend telling people five positive things for every comment that could possibly be interpreted as negative – so in effect, you are operating on a ratio of 5 to 1 in positive versus ambiguous or less-than-positive communications.

Epilogue to the Second Print Edition

Why? Because too many leaders don't spend enough time giving positive feedback. Some say nothing at all until they need to comment or correct something that a subordinate or colleague is doing wrong. Over time, this pattern causes others to feel unappreciated and so defensive that when you approach them, they know that you are unhappy with them. Is that good leadership?

In contrast, be on the lookout for good things and call attend to them in positive ways. When someone on your staff sends you a well written and informative email, for example, take a few seconds to reply and tell them that. But let me suggest going even a little further. Instead of just replying "good email," explain why it was good. Maybe your staffer took the time to provide extra data or information that saved you time, for example, or organized information clearly, or provided a little background that deepened your understanding of what was going on.

If they did that, say that. It is a small revision and addition to your leadership approach, but I predict that it can increase your effectiveness far more than you expect. If you apply it consistently, your people will be happier, more motivated and less distracted by worry. Please try it and again, let me know how it has helped you.

APPENDIX A

Track Your Action Steps and Get Started

CHAPTER THREE

ACTION STEP: Think of an issue that you are facing in your company – a problem that you are trying to solve. Try to dig deeper and deeper down until you have identified all the possible root causes of it. Then decide which of them to address first, and how. Remember that other people will be able to offer you a wider range of perspectives and suggestions than you can generate if you attempt to solve the problem on your own.

ACTION STEP: Reflect on how you talk to people and request their ideas and help. Do you take the time to explain the issue you are facing? Do you check to ensure that they understand why you are asking? Do you leave an opening for them to suggest better ideas and solutions?

ACTION STEP: Over the next few days, consciously take time to ask people for more help. Consider their reactions. Over time, evaluate how your relationships with those people have improved.

ACTION STEP: Reflect on areas in which you may have become complacent.

ACTION STEP: Review how you have collaborated on specific tasks and projects in the past. Did you involve the right people? If you could attack the same issue or challenge again, would you invite the same people to collaborate with you? If not, whom would you invite instead?

ACTION STEP: Pinpoint a large project or initiative that you have been delaying. Make a list of small first "bites" you can take that can get the process started, and then take action on one of them.

Track Your Action Steps and Get Started

CHAPTER FOUR

ACTION STEP: Take some time and review the factors that create company culture. Where does your current company culture belong among these categories? Where would you like it to be? What changes will you make to get there?

ACTION STEP: Reflect on the business you are in and make a list of predictions about the changes that are about to happen in your industry in the next five years.

ACTION STEP: Bring your company's story and history back to life and use it to inspire and ingage people. Was your organization started by an interesting individual to meet an unusual need in the marketplace? Are there certain big events in your company's past that reflect its core values or tell the stories of big new successes? If so, talk about them, make them part of your training programs and roll them into an effective "elevator speech" that informs and inspires.

CHAPTER FIVE

ACTION STEPS: Over the next two days, pay attention to times when people state opinions as facts. Watch some commentary shows on television and notice when it's taking place. Pay attention to your own communication too, and try to make sure that others know when you are stating an opinion. What do these steps tell you about how effectively you and other people in your organization make this important distinction?

ACTION STEP: Talk to some trusted friends to determine if you are a good listener. Rather than asking them whether your listening skills are good, ask some open-ended questions like, "After we have discussed something, do you feel as though I have heard you out, or do you still have ideas that you were not able to air?" or, "When you are speaking, do I allow you enough time and space to fully explain what is on your mind?" After those open-ended questions, consider asking something more direct, like, "Can you recommend two or three specific things I could do if I wanted to become a better listener?

Track Your Action Steps and Get Started

CHAPTER SIX

ACTION STEPS: When have you been evasive and why? What was the result? Remember, there are times when withholding information can be practical. It is not necessary to share every detail of information in every situation, after all. Be aware, however, that people who are habitually evasive – who constantly try to "cover their backs" – can do a lot of harm to your organization.

ACTION STEP: Think of a conversation you had when you were conclusive – and when you could have benefitted from being more open and honest. If you could now repeat that talk at a higher level, how might the results have differed?

Ingaging Leadership

CHAPTER SEVEN

ACTION STEP: Consider the variety of the people in your company. Are there gaps in ability, attitude or experience that are preventing your organization from achieving its greatest potential? If you were starting up today, what kind of staff would allow the business to grow and prosper?

ACTION STEP: Identify several employees in your organization who would benefit if you created development plans for them. Next, write down some of the steps that you would include in that plan, such as training, spending time in other company locations, and more. After that, try to identify more employees who could benefit if you created a plan for each of them. Finally, make some decisions about whether, when and how you might create those plans.

ACTION STEP: Identify some areas in your organization where training could have the potential to improve performance dramatically. Make a plan to provide it.

Track Your Action Steps and Get Started

ACTION STEP: Assess the way your organization conducts reviews. Consider regularity, approach, methodology, and look for areas ripe for improvements.

ACTION STEP: Review your benefits plan by comparing it to those that are being offered by other companies where your employees could be looking for jobs. If your benefits aren't in the ballpark, you could be encouraging your people to leave you.

ACTION STEP: I recently attended an excellent presentation by Jeremy McKinley, a very smart man who is a member of the top marketing team at Trek Bicycle. He was discussing his strategies for marketing and brand success. One of his slides said simply, "Fire Someone – You Know Who It Is."

EPILOGUE

ACTION STEP: Try using the Three Things exercise for at least a month. I strongly recommend it. It has resulted in great change in in family and in the lives of other people who have tried it. I predict it will do the same for you.

ACTION STEP: Download the free Study Guide at Ingage.com and start discussing Ingaging Leadership within your company. Don't just focus on senior leadership, share this book with an inspiring leader in your company and see what happens. After you have explored this book, go on to study *The Energy Bus* by Jon Gordon and *The Fred Factor* by Marc Sanborn.

Acknowledgements

I want to thank and acknowledge so many people for the roles they have played in my life and in the creation of this book. Without their knowledge, support and inspiration, I would never have become the person I am today and I would certainly never have undertaken to put my thoughts down on paper.

First, I want to thank my wife Laura for her love and support of our entire family and me. A true life partner, she shares my eagerness to learn to be a better leader. Laura has been with me at seminars at the Center for Authentic Leadership and elsewhere, discussing concepts with me at all hours and helping to deepen my understanding of leadership. She is a remarkably successful businesswoman too. She joined Cambridge Technology Partners early in her career when it was a relatively small, $9 million company. During her tenure, it grew to a billion-dollar company, with a lot of the credit going to her work there in many roles, including Senior VP for Human Resources. I have never known anyone who can equal her ability to create a safe and caring space where people can interact. She has built success on success, thanks in part to her empathy for others at every stage. She is now owner of Artful Healings, an inspiring company that helps people gain health through traditional healing arts. I know that many adventures lie ahead for us.

I want to give special thanks to my mother and late father, Sonya and Paul, who passed away at the time when I was completing this book. My father was a unique man, the former owner of a small business that he ran with vision, passion, and the highest of standards. He was widely respected, the kind of man for whom people would do anything. When I was only 10 years old, he let me start to work in the family business and from that age I began to learn how to manage a business. (How many people are privileged to have that kind of experience from such an early age?) My mother is just as remarkable, a woman of incredible strength and conviction of opinion. Without her devotion to me, I would probably never have graduated from high school, let alone college. When I needed someone to step up and advocate for me, she was always there and never let me down.

Special thanks go to my very different, very wonderful children Aaron, Alex and Alton. I expect that it has not always been completely easy for them to have a dad who has been so busy working, traveling and claiming time to take

Acknowledgements

part in a committed study of leadership. My thanks and love go to them every day.

Thanks go equally to my sisters Shira and Nina, and to my brother John. They have all been such a great part of my life. As a businesswoman, Nina was been nothing short of an inspiration, entering the business world as a technology saleswoman at a time when the field was almost completely dominated by men.

I offer profound appreciation and thanks to Alan Greenburg and Howard Brodsky, the co-CEOs of CCA Global Partners. I started working there in 1988 when the company was called Carpet Co-op of America. I was only the fifth employee on the payroll. These two men placed their trust in me completely and gave me the opportunity to learn and grow. They let me start a marketing department, introduce a training division, and launch a variety of new enterprises that included an international design group, new franchise operations and new initiatives that included a co-op that issues $65 billion in mortgages and even a formalwear company. During my 20 years at CCA, we achieved an average annual growth rate of 29% compounded. By the time I left the company, I had achieved $5 billion in system-wide sales and was responsible for 70% of the firm's overall profitability. I accomplished a lot, but none of it would have been possible without the vision and support of these two men, who are like brothers to me.

I want to acknowledge Jan Smith, the inspiring leader who founded the Center for Authentic Leadership in 1985. The Future Thinking and Leadership Intensive programs that she created led me to discover new vistas of ingaged and visionary leadership. The three levels of communication that I write about in this book are based in part on the Communication Meter that she created, and I thank her for that.

I offer great thanks to the remarkable people at both Ingage Consulting and Tortal Consultants. I have learned so much from all of you and often been inspired by your insights and tireless work. I wish to offer special thanks to Deb Binder (a woman who is so wonderful that I have actually hired her on three different occasions) and Cordell Riley, who brings unequalled insight into the world of franchising in the automotive sector. Great thanks also go to all members of the Ingage team, including Marcia Hewey, Janet Brideaux, Stephanie Stiles, Danny P. Kagan, Mike Ziglar, Dan Black, Joshua R. De La Vega, and Matthew Cole. Still more thanks go to Aaron Chase and all the members of his great team at Tortal Consultants.

Thanks also go to Ellen Liberman, a brilliant and incisive editor who reviewed this manuscript before publication and offered many helpful ideas. Her comments and suggestions made this book more readable, more insightful, and much more positive in tone.

Finally, I want to thank Barry Lenson, the editor and business journalist who helped me organize my ideas and

Track Your Action Steps and Get Started

put them together into this book. He listened and talked to me for many hours. Along the way, we laughed, exchanged opinions and ideas, and enjoyed one of the more productive collaborations that I can recall.

About the Author

Evan Hackel is a franchise industry leader, a widely published writer, a keynote speaker, a member of the New England Franchise Association Board, and Co-Chair of the International Franchise Association's Knowledge Share Task Force.

A consultant to some of the largest franchise systems in North America, Evan is also Founder and Principal of Ingage Consulting, a consulting firm focused on improving the performance of franchises and all business organizations. By building cultures of partnership and common purpose within organizations, Ingage Consulting has established a record of helping a variety of organizations dramatically improve performance. In addition, Evan serves as CEO of Tortal Training, a firm that specializes in developing interactive eLearning solutions for companies in all sectors.

Before founding Ingage Consulting, Evan worked at CCA Global Partners for twenty years. At CCA, he was responsible for four business divisions with over 2000 units, over $5 billion in sales operating in four countries. He also founded CCA's departments in marketing, national programs, and training. He led the company's effort to buy and turn around a franchise organization from bankruptcy. In four years he grew the troubled franchise from 250 locations to a very successful with more than 550 locations.

Evan received an MBA from Boston College and a BA in Economics from Colorado College. He is a current and former board member of several organizations, cooperatives and groups to which he lends his expertise. He resides in Reading, Massachusetts with his wife, Laura, and three children.

About Ingage Consulting

Ingage Consulting, headquartered in Woburn, Massachusetts, is the foremost provider of specialized management consulting services for leaders of franchises, cooperatives, buying groups and dealer networks. Drawing directly from his leadership experience at a number of business cooperatives and group organizations, Founder and Principal Evan Hackel works to make his client organizations more successful from the inside out by bolstering organizational ingagement, empowerment and collaboration.

Who we are *(mission)*

We are ingagement champions.

What we do *(purpose)*

We help our clients succeed, by building strong, ingaged organizations.

Where we're going *(vision)*

Acknowledged for being the thought leader on business ingagement.

Our core values include:

- **Collaboration** - We involve as many stakeholders as we can from organizations to identify the problem and brainstorm solutions. Similarly, we involve the right people from our team.

- **Openness** - We value honesty and truthfulness, and as such we are known for telling it as it is.

- **Listening** - The only way you can fully appreciate a person's perspective is by listening to him or her.

- **Understanding** - We strive to know the big picture, to put the puzzle together before deconstructing it to make it better. Innovation: we anticipate what people need, and always look for new and different solutions to problems.

- **Focusing on results** - We are driven to improve the performance of your business and achieve your business goals.

How we get there *(direction)*

We are life-long learners, and are committed to constantly evolving and getting better at what we do.

About Ingage Consulting

We believe our organization needs to exemplify everything we help our customers achieve. As such, we hire people who share our values and strategic direction, and offer them a great place to work.

We publish and openly share best practices. We are educators, not just consultants of the industry.

We grow our business organically, through acquisition and by aligning with like-minded companies.

Ingage Consulting
400 Trade Center
Suite 5900
Woburn MA 01801-7472
TEL: (781) 281-9390

About Tortal Training

Tortal Training, headquartered in Charlotte, North Carolina, is a full-service training and development firm that specializes in developing interactive eLearning solutions. Tortal Training is the only training service partner that uses strategic ingagement methodologies. This helps organizations with distributed workforces leverage their talent development to maximize training effectiveness and drive sustainable business results.

Customers choose Tortal Training over the competition to get training that works. By tying increased ingagement to all products and services, Tortal Training has the ability to set itself apart from DIY options, LMS companies and even internal capabilities through customer education and demonstrated effectiveness.

Tortal also offers online training solutions, speakers' services and a range of additional services in the training sector.

Tortal Training has achieved remarkable success for clients from a number of industries that include advanced manufacturing, automotive, commercial cleaning, emergency cleaning, healthcare, hair salons, food service, home organization, painting, personal fitness and gyms, property damage remediation, rent-to-own, and retail.

Tortal Training
14825 Ballantyne Village Way
Building A, Suite 240-4
Charlotte, NC 28277
TK ADD TELEPHONE

About Ingaging Leadership...

Ingagement is a philosophy for leaders who believe that it is not enough to tell people what to do, but to ingage their minds, creativity and even their emotions and their hearts.

Ingaged leadership starts with a belief that when you align people and create an organization where everyone works together in partnership, that organization becomes vastly more successful.

As you will discover in Ingaging Leadership, ingagement isn't a single action that you take just once. It is an ongoing, dynamic business practice that has the power to transform your organization, your people, you, and ultimately, your success.

Please Tell Me More

Because I am hoping that you and I can grow together as leaders, I invite you to send me further comments and suggestions to me at ehackel@ingage.net.

Index

Assumptions, 90, 97
Attitude, employee, 124–125
Attitude, hiring for, 123
Benefit plans, 132–134
CCA Global Partners, ix, 25-26, 31, 34-35, 153, 163
Chipotle, 77-78
Coaching, 40, 74
Collaboration, 42, 55
Communication, best practices, 63, 85, 89, 101–116
Communication, three levels of, 101–116
Company cultures, 68–74
Company values, 138
Complacency, fighting, 52–54
Convention attendance, building, 27–28
Corporate culture, 68–74
Engagement Ratio (Gallup), 19–22
Facts vs. opinions, communicating, 59, 93–96
Flooring America, ix, 24–27
Framing of problems, 49
Franchise Business Review, 23
Fresh perspectives, asking for, 50–51
Gallup Organization, 19–22, 119–120
Healthcare, employee plans, 132–134
Help, asking for, 46–48

Hiring, 73, 121–123, 135–137
Honesty, 105, 110, 111–114, 135
Ingage Barometer (analytical tool), 23–24
Ingage Consulting, 4, 154, 157, 159–161
Input, asking for, 16, 29, 51–52, 55, 57–58, 63
Job reviews, 92, 126, 128–132
Key performance indicators, 47–48
Liminality Inc., 23
Listening skills, 14–16, 99, 108, 135, 148
Lying, 96, 104–107, 115
Mission statements, 75–77, 81–82
Mistakes, 56, 59, 121
People, investing in, 125–126
Performance indicators, key, 47–48
Planning, 28, 77–79
Problems, attacking the causes of, 12–13, 40–42
Recruiting employees, 73, 117, 120–125
Repeat customers, cultivating, 40

Reviews, employee, 92, 126, 128–132
Sales and selling, 40, 43–45
Staffing, 117–123
Strategic planning, 28, 77–79
Terminations, employee, 135
Training, 127, 132, 133, 134, 149, 163–164
Underlying cause of problems, 40–42
Vision statements, 76–77
Work-life balance, 54

CPSIA information can be obtained
at www.ICGtesting.com
Printed in the USA
BVOW06*2104260117
474525BV00004B/4/P